TIMING THE MARKET

How To Profit in Bull and Bear Markets With Technical Analysis

by
Curtis M. Arnold
Dan Rahfeldt
Weiss Research, Inc.

EDITED BY MARTIN D. WEISS
Weiss Research, Inc.

PROBUS PUBLISHING

Chicago, Illinois

This publication is designed to provide accurate and authoritative information in regard to the subject matter covered. It is sold with the understanding that the publisher is not engaged in rendering legal, accounting or other professional service. If legal advice or other expert assistance is required, the services of a competent professional person should be sought.

Portions of this book appeared previously in *Your Personal Computer Can Make You Rich in Stocks and Commodities,* published by Weiss Research, Inc.

FROM A DECLARATION OF PRINCIPLES JOINTLY ADOPTED BY A COMMITTEE OF THE AMERICAN BAR ASSOCIATION AND A COMMITTEE OF PUBLISHERS.

Library of Congress Cataloging-in-Publication Data

Arnold, Curtis M.
  Timing the market.

  Includes index.
  1. Investment analysis.   2. Investments.
I. Rahfeldt, Dan.   II. Weiss, Martin D.   III. Title.
HG4529.A76 1986   332.63'2   86-5056
ISBN 0-917253-37-X (case)
ISBN 0-917253-96-5 (pbk)

Printed in the United States of America

4   5   6   7   8   9   0

TABLE OF CONTENTS

PART IV CYCLES

PART V COMMODITY MARKETS

PREFACE

Whether you're interested in stocks or commodities, whether you believe that prices are going up or down, it has been proven time and time again that the most reliable method for timing the markets is technical analysis.

The problem is that most investors think it's best left to professionals— people who are willing to wade through a room full of charts and graphs ... consult all sorts of esoteric, quasi-mystical indicators ... and maybe throw a dart at the board on the sly. *Nothing could be further from the truth!*

Technical analysis is simply a method for forecasting market trends and timing critical turns—for generating specific buy or sell signals based on readily obtainable information. It's accurate, unemotional and *very profitable.* Moreover, now, for the first time, it's well within your grasp. You should read this book if:

* You have an interest in making every dollar you invest produce maximum profits, with minimal risk.

* You invest in any market, anywhere in the world, including stocks, bonds, futures, precious metals, real estate, rare coins or tangibles; puts and calls, mutual funds, money funds and more.

* You're either an active or a passive investor.

* You're a seasoned professional or an absolute beginner.

* You want to control your investments, rather than your investments (or someone else) controlling you.

* You realize that others, no smarter than you, are making fortunes utilizing the modern principles of technical analysis.

This book has much to offer you, today, tomorrow, and long into the future. Starting with the history of the very first individuals who recognized the value of unemotional, empirical analysis of market data ... and continuing through the entire current spectrum of techniques, market indicators, their profitable application, and their underlying principles ... you'll be guided along the road that leads to real comprehension of technical analysis.

You'll learn virtually effortlessly, about charts and graphs, everything about a myriad of technical indicators, how to construct your own technical system and, most importantly, how to profitably interpret the results.

Technical analysis is not merely a set of rules and formulas that you learn once and then put into practice. It represents the collective experiences of thousands of traders who made, and often lost, huge sums of money over the years.

PROLOGUE:

THE SECRETS OF THE PAST

Imagine that we are back in the early part of this century. Much like today, market volatility is tremendous, trading volume is on the rise And, as in today's futures markets, small losers are everywhere; but large winners are few and far between.

Who are they? Where can we find them? As we shall soon see, they are a small handful of traders who were flying into the face of conventional wisdom, ignoring the strict fundamental principles of their time, and developing their own unique technically-based theories and trading systems.

We walk into the second-floor offices of a small, smoked-filled brokerage firm. The floor is littered with the debris of thousands of trades and streams of ticker tape. We discover that the real technical analyst is not the "customer's man" behind his desk or the senior partners in the back offices. Rather he is the 14-year old boy scurrying to post the numbers on the quotation board while another clerk, sitting by the ticker, calls out the prices. His name: Jesse Livermore.

Having a good memory for figures, he begins to detect certain patterns in the behavior of stock prices before they embark on an advance or decline. We follow him through adulthood, and we see that, by perfecting his tape-reading into a science, and by putting up only 10% margin, he is able to multiply his capital many times—so much so that he is eventually trading huge blocks of stock. This gives him the ability to "test" the market before he commits himself heavily.

You ask: "I don't get it, Jesse. How do you do it?" "Here's how it works: If I want to buy a stock, I will first start selling into the market. If the price doesn't go down, I conclude that there's good support for that stock at that level, that it's safe to buy. Conversely, if the stock's price does go down easily, I'll continue selling it, driving the price down still further until it can find support."

"But how can you tell?"

"From the volume, from the price action, from the rhythm of the ticker. You can *feel* when you're touching bottom."

This is both fascinating and disappointing. You know that in today's massive markets, you will never be able to "test the markets" like Livermore did. They're simply too big. But you make a mental note to yourself that when you get into this book on technical analysis you will pay close attention to the many techniques that use his basic principles. You will seek to quantify them in a way that you can readily comprehend and profitably utilize ... even if you're not blessed with Jesse's intuitive genius.

Our next stop is the home of a man by the name of W. D. Gann. As he opens the door to invite us in, we are struck by the obvious contrast in his style and approach. Livermore was a hands-on practitioner who learned his techniques during market hours. This man is a tireless student who pours over his charts into the wee hours of the morning. "What stocks do you own right now, Mr. Gann?" "Stocks? Own?" comes the puzzled response. "None!" You later discover that he is about to complete ten years of research on over one hundred years of stock market fluctuations—both in the U.S. and in England—before making his first investment. His homework certainly pays off. Legend has it that he eventually amasses over $50 million from his speculations in stocks and commodities.

"The basis of market movements," he asserts, "can be found in natural laws. You may think I'm crazy. But this is why I have spent so many years studying astrology, numerology, and the great pyramids. Here, look at this! See these diagrams? They show the common link that is all-pervasive—the importance of time, cycles, and seasonality."

"Yes, but, how can you use that to make money in the stock market?" He smiles. "Gentlemen. Stocks, like atoms, are the centers of energies which are controlled *mathematically.* In other words, the Law of Vibration can help to accurately determine the exact points to which stocks or commodities should rise and fall within a certain time frame. Learn those laws of nature. Plot their time and space coordinates on your charts. And more often than not, you will be able to predict the future with amazing accuracy."

You're not convinced. You wonder if this is more mysticism than science. So you spend days and months pouring over his actual forecasts. You are shocked to discover that the forecasts are too accurate to be attributed to sheer luck or coincidence. Later, however, when we return to 1986 and try to apply his knowledge to today's markets you will find that no one is able to duplicate his incredible results. You will be occasionally frustrated by the flagrant ambiguities that permeate his work, and you may begin to wonder that perhaps Gann never did reveal—to us or to anyone else—his ultimate discoveries.

You are heartened, however, by one fact: Even though his successes cannot be duplicated, others have taken great inspiration from Gann's work and gone on to develop valuable technical tools of their own. Like them, you are inspired by his belief that nothing is too farfetched or too insignificant to bear investigation and further research ... regardless of how often others ridicule your novel notions.

For now, however, you're anxious to get down to some really straightforward analysis. So we take you to a man by the name of Richard D. Wyckoff. At first, he reminds us a bit of Jesse Livermore; he's a consummate tape-reader. "The future course of prices," he tells us, "can be determined by a careful analysis of volume which, when combined with the skills of tape-reading, give you a solid three-dimensional picture of the market. The key to your success will be to seek out—and then act upon—the *patterns of accumulation and distribution. Do not act unless you are prepared.*"

"In what sense?" We inquire.

"Anyone who buys or sells a stock, a bond or a commodity for profit is speculating if he employs intelligent foresight. If he does not, he is gambling. But never place blind faith in any one system. Stock market technique is not, and never will be an exact science. Stock prices are made by the minds of men. Whatever technical analysis you do, remember that you—and not your technique—are the boss ... with discipline and without emotion, of course. Breaking your own rules is like cheating at solitaire. But, no matter how good your technique, you will still needs a healthy dose of human judgement for your final decision."

"OK. But what *is* your technique? Tell us exactly how you go about picking a bottom." He leans back in his chair as you prepare yourself for a detailed explanation. "Here. Let me run through it step by step: Remember, you must watch out for accumulation. Look for a period of several months of lateral movement at the bottom of a downwave. That's when large traders are gradually buying in the face of negative sentiment and selling by the public." Wyckoff pauses.

"Is that it?" you ask. "No. In fact, I believe I have actually identified six distinct price/volume behavior patterns which occur during the accumulation process. First, there's what I call 'preliminary support' on a day when you see a marked increase in volume and a temporary halt to the decline. Second, you'll usually get a resumption in the downtrend and what I call a 'selling climax' on extremely heavy volume. But watch out for one *minor* detail of *major* importance: Towards the end of that day, prices bounce up to close significantly above the lows of the day. Third, you can start looking for an *automatic* rally which results from short-covering. Fourth, prices eventually *retest the low* of the selling climax on lighter volume. This is your *secondary test*. A trading range follows which may last several months. Eventually, prices rally strongly off the lows of the trading range on heavy volume. This is your first real *sign of strength*. The next correction has very narrow daily ranges. It's the *last point of support* and your last chance to get in before the new uptrend begins. Finally, once an uptrend has been completed, you will probably see a similar but inverted pattern near the top—during *distribution*."

You lean over and whisper. "Aha! Now we have something concrete, something we can sink our teeth into. Let's start rolling with real money!"

Wait a minute! This is just one example of the many concepts contributed by technical analysts reviewed in this book. Besides, before we return to our time, we have one last stop to make in the 1930s—to talk to a gentleman by the name of R. H. Elliot.

"They say I'm a revolutionary or some kind of crackpot, but some day I think people will find my theory quite rational. (In fact, it later will be known as Elliot Wave Theory). Here's what I've discovered: Specific patterns in price movement are caused by swings in mass investor psychology—from pessimism to optimism and back again. I have identified thirteen distinct patterns into which all stock market movements can be classified."

"You mean time and cycles like in Gann's work?" we ask. "Not exactly. I place more credence in the *formations* that prices exhibit on charts. The stock market, indeed, any market, unfolds according to a basic rhythm or pattern of *five waves up* and *three waves down*. The three waves down are a correction of the preceding five waves up. But that's not all. There is a precise proportionate relationship—in time and magnitude—between the distances traveled during each of the waves. I call it the *Golden Ratio*. Some people are vaguely aware of these waves and call them "thrusts" or simply "moves." But they don't know how to count them; they can't seem to tell where one ends and the other begins; and most important, they don't realize that the waves are often related to one another by the Golden Ratio of.618—a ratio which, by the way, is also found in the growth of snails, the logarithmic expansion of the universe and the Great Pyramids."

When we return to the present time, you wonder out loud: "What good has it done us to discover the techniques that worked fifty years ago? Aren't markets totally different today?"

To which we respond: "Yes, on the surface, they are, and our ability to track and quantify them is certainly superior. But the basic forces that drove prices up and down in previous generations are still at work today. All markets—both then and now—are simply auctions; and all auctions, no matter what the technology, are governed by the same general principles of supply and demand. The price of a stock or commodity today, as in the past, mirrors investors' expectations of the future—their collective emotions of hope, fear, and greed. It is the ability of technical analysis to identify and predict these future perceptions of value that makes it such a valuable tool."

If you want to be a writer, you read Shakespeare, Dickens, and Twain. Likewise, if you want to do technical analysis, you must study Livermore, Gann, Wyckoff, Elliot, Dow, and others. This is not just because they are "the classics," but also because most modern-day technical analysts have incorporated many of their trading·techniques. In this chapter, we have seen only a capsulized glimpse into their market theories. It's by no means enough to do justice to their great works. But we hope it will whet your appetite to explore their ideas more fully. In any case, subsequent chapters of this book review many of today's major technical indicators, most of which have their "roots" firmly planted in the past of these pioneers.

I

HOW TO PROFIT
FROM TECHNICAL ANALYSIS

1

TWO ROADS TO SUCCESS

IN THE MARKETS

The time is the second half of the 1980s. Stretched out before you are the widest diversity of markets, with the most powerful leverage and the greatest opportunities—*or dangers*—in all economic history. You are both bewildered and fascinated by the speed of change and the plethora of technical indicators used to track that change.

However, before you can move into this new, often unchartered territory, you come to a series of crossroads, where you must make some basic decisions regarding how you will approach the markets in general.

At the first crossroad you are confronted by a stranger who asks you: "Do you want to be a *picker* or a *follower*?"

"What do you mean?"

"The pickers are all those that try to pick a bottom or pick a top. They say that they have technical tools which will predict the next market turn, help them get in before it really makes its move and get out just before it heads back in the other direction. For lack of a better term, we call them '*bottom-pickers*' and '*top-pickers.*'

But more often than not, they're the ones who, in effect, get picked off ... like flies."

"Every time there's the slightest rally or correction, you can hear them shouting 'this is it! Now's the time to buy (or sell).' Granted, there are some who do make money, but for the most part they suffer from what we call the ICGAL syndrome—that die-hard belief that "It Can't Go Any Lower."

The stranger points towards the horizon. "See over yonder. That's where you'll find the ceremonial burial ground of the thousands of would-be traders who literally got killed trying to pick " the bottom" in copper, lumber, sugar, gold, crude oil and virtually every commodity imaginable. Some of them actually had a better-than-normal batting average. But they bounced in and out of the markets so often, their equity got eaten alive by commissions, even discount commissions.

"The *followers* use a somewhat more conservative approach. Rather than trying to catch the entire move, from top to bottom, their brand of technical analysis is geared to giving them *confirmation* that the market is indeed trending in one direction or another. Then, and only then, do they jump on board. So they're the *trend-followers*."

"So what's so bad about that?"

"Nothing at all. Trouble is, more often than not, by the time they get in, the market has *already* moved substantially and is ripe for a correction, a sudden reversal in the opposite direction. Often the followers stick it out for a while until their losses are unbearable. Then they bail out just before the market is ready to move their way again. In the final analysis, what many wind up doing is exactly the opposite of what they should be doing; they buy near the top and sell near the bottom! You can find *their* burial ground adjacent to that of the *pickers*."

You're discouraged. Is this is what it's all about? Losing money left and right, getting decimated by choppy, unpredictable markets where nothing works? For many, the answer is yes. It's not for lack of technical tools, though. It's because they commit one or more of the cardinal errors of investing.

Three Fatal Errors

Error #1. They overtrade. They're too anxious to always *do* something and they do it with too many shares or contracts. Several years from now, if you remember nothing else from this book, do remember this:

Trade consistently in *modest* amounts so you can always stay cool and unemotional about any particular trade.

Error #2. They are overly influenced by what they hear or see outside of their own technical work. Even the most seasoned professionals can fall prey to this malady. It's only natural; humans are social animals. But to be successful, you must act independently, as a loner. If you listen to someone else, he may get you in at the right time, but will he be there to tell you when to get out?

We believe you should either make *all* of the decisions or you should make *none* of the decisions by employing a money manager with a good track record. If you bought this book, we assume you have chosen the former, at least for a portion of your funds.

Error #3. They don't have a simple set of procedures, or if they do, they don't follow them. The indicators in this book are the building blocks for you to build your system—trading rules that you can follow without ambiguity. Once you have such a system, try it out on paper for a few months. Then trade token amounts. And finally, if it works to your satisfaction, shift into full gear. But do not arbitrarily, because of fear, greed or any other reason, break your own rules. By trading modestly, you can afford to stick with your system until it either proves itself or bombs out. If you change course midstream, however, you will never know for sure.

The Spider Strategy

The fact is that, although there are many small losers in the markets, there are also a small number of very large winners! You *can* pick tops and bottoms. But to do so successfully, you must follow what we call **the spider strategy**. The spider does not need to "feed" every day. He is content to wait until a morsel comes his way, patient and secure in the knowledge that he has taken the steps necessary for his survival.

His carefully crafted web transmits to him all sorts of information. But he knows how to identify the false signals—the wind vibrating his web, a drop of rain—from the real thing enmeshed in it. Why does he know it so intimately? Because he has carefully constructed his web himself. No one else can build it for him. As a result, the configuration of his web is as uniquely his as his finger prints. Most important, the spider is patient. He waits until he sees a *convergence* of most or all of his indicators before he acts; but when he does, he pounces aggressively and without hesitation.

If you follow this strategy, you will use, among others, those indicators which tell you when a market is "overbought" and vulnerable to a decline, or conversely when it is "oversold" and ripe for a move up. These are the so-called "oscillators"—the indicators that oscillate back and forth, like an electrocardiogram, from the top and the bottom of a predefined range.

One of the most common of these is **momentum** which measures and plots the net change from one period to the next. Imagine the pendulum on a grandfather clock, swinging from one extreme to another with a momentum that carries it as far as it can go in one direction ... before reversing to the other direction. The same is true for markets.

The Omnipresent Approach

You can also make money trend-following. Here however you must employ what we call the *omnipresent* approach. In other words, you have to maintain small positions in many different markets at all times. You must be willing to go short (more on short selling later) any market that is trending down and buy any market that's trending up, not hesitating to reverse your positions when the market reverses. You will absolutely need—at all times—a diversified portfolio. (Stocks alone cannot give you enough diversification, no matter how many different industries you're in!) Your portfolio should have at least one position in each major market sector—not only stocks, but also precious metals, bonds, foreign currencies, agricultural commodities, etc.

Most important, in order to win with trend-following, you must be willing to accept a large number of relatively small losses in order to stay on board for a small number of very large gains. During choppy sideways periods, you must have enough money in the kitty to with-stand a steady erosion in your equity. And during big moves, you need the courage to stay with your position until your trend-following system tells you to get out, no matter how anxious you may be to grab a profit. In this book you will find several methods for trend-following, among which moving averages are probably the most common and easy to use.

Remember, although helter-skelter trend-following is indeed hazardous, with a systematic and disciplined approach you will indeed make money using this approach. There will be ups and there will be downs. But as long as you steer clear of the three cardinal errors, you should wind up with substantial profits in most years.

Before you get too deeply into technical analysis you will come to one more crossroad. You see a signpost just ahead with a question in bold letters ...

2

TO COMPUTE OR NOT TO COMPUTE

While that decision is both personal and economic, please allow us to make one major point: a computer is nothing but a fast pencil; and neither will make you a penny in the markets if you don't use them!

Let there be no doubt. All of the great pioneers of technical analysis did their work completely without the benefit of a computer. For example:

Charles Dow. He died in 1902, so we think we can safely rule out any possibility that he used computers. The great Russian economist/cycle analyst Kondratieff ... who perished in a prison camp somewhere in Mongolia. We seriously doubt that they furnished him with an IBM PC or an APPLE IIe!

Perhaps one of the best current examples would be Joe Granville ... he got his great inspiration for his "On Balance Volume" theory while sitting in the bathroom of a major brokerage firm in New York in the early 60s. An electric hand-dryer? Maybe. But we assure you there wasn't a computer in sight! On the other hand there are many who might say that the computer has done for technical analysis what the Gutenberg printing press did for the printed word.

Have you ever asked yourself questions such as these: In the last ten years, if you had bought silver on each new moon and sold it on the full moon, would you have made money? In the last two years, if you bought the S + P 500 Index at each Thursday's close and sold it at each Monday's open, what would the results have been? Technical analysts of the past rarely asked these types of questions—not so much because they appear to be irrelevant—but primarily because they didn't have the time, energy and, frankly, the means, to find the answers. Today, the speed of the computer makes answering "what if" questions like these a breeze. It's simply a matter of historical testing or "simulation."

What do *we* think about all this? Very simple: Technical analysis can be performed *with* or *without* a computer. What computers have accomplished is primarily to help you with the "grunt work"—to eliminate much of the drudgery with mathematical calculations required to apply some of today's more popular analytical techniques.

A personal computer will allow you to track a far broader range of indicators in a much larger universe of markets, increasing many times the number of good choices available to you. In addition, there are certain kinds of analysis that require so many calculations, doing them by hand would be very difficult. For these reasons we do recommend you seriously consider computers as a tool for expanding your technical analysis horizons. (For more information, see the Reader Services page in the back of this book.)

The day is fast approaching when computers will be able to learn from experience. But to date, we know of no such system that can compete effectively with a rational and thinking human who systematically uses a variety of indicators. If you do decide to use computers, there is a wide variety of easy-to-use programs available, especially on the IBM PC or compatible machines and on the Apple. Remember, however, that your computer is 100% neutral on the markets—neither an optimist always looking for prices to go up (a "bull") nor a pessimist that lies in wait for the day when prices go down (a "bear"). In other words, it has neither a "bullish" nor a "bearish" bias. You are still the one who has to make the critical decisions to buy or to sell.

Are you now ready to plunge ahead? Not quite. If you are going to learn how to profit from technical analysis, you will want to know why technical analysis works. What is it that makes the market go up or down?"

3

WHY TECHNICAL ANALYSIS WORKS

There are several schools of thought. One school believes in the theory behind **chart formations and patterns.** They read charts much like ancient astrologers read the stars, looking for "head and shoulders" formations; an "M" or a "W"; "wedges," "flags" and "pennants." These, they believe, reflect the patterns of buying and selling, accumulation and distribution, or market psychology.

Others have demonstrated that these formations are merely the sum total of various **cycles.** Edward R. Dewey, perhaps the preeminent cycle researcher and analyst of this or any other century, defined them as "the tendency of events to repeat themselves at more or less uniform intervals ... the pulsations of distant stars ... the prevalence of sunspots ... weather conditions ... the abundance of mammals, birds, insects and fish, and the prices of securities."

The big problem however is this: Which cycle is now impacting the market? The temperature reading at 12 noon on February 8th is determined by a convergence of cycles of different length—the 24-hour cycle of the earth rotating on its own axis, the 12-month cycle of the rotation around the sun, and longer-term weather cycles which may be as long as 50 years or more, and so forth. The same goes for markets, except it's not always so clear which cycle is now in force.

Finally, some of the most successful traders are those that use **market sentiment.** The theory is that if too many people are **bullish** (optimistic) about the market going up, the market is ripe for a decline as they take profits or are forced to get out. Conversely, if too many are **bearish** (pessimistic), it implies an up move may be in the making.

R. Earl Hadady's organization, publishers of *Bullish Consensus (Market Vane),* is in the forefront of this type of research. A wide range of investment advisors and analysts are polled every week for their views on virtually every market. These data are then compiled with a formula which factors in (a) how strongly the advisor feels about each market and (b) how many followers he or she has. (See page 175 for details.)

W.O.W. Indexes

At Weiss Research, we have added one further dimension to the study of market sentiment by tracking Who Owns What **(W.O.W)**. W.O.W is based on this principle: Whether you're talking about stocks, bonds, precious metals, foreign currencies or commodities, there is one fact which is virtually immutable: If it's held by **strong hands,** the likelihood of a sudden bout of selling is greatly reduced. Any news, whether normally interpreted as "good" or "bad," will tend to trigger a rise. If it's held by **weak hands,** the most likely move will be down.

In this book we present various methods for timing the markets. However, our personal view is this: *The key to timing the markets is accurately tracking the strong hands vs. the weak hands—what they own and when, in what relative proportions and, perhaps most important, how this critical "market composition" is changing from one month to the next.*

But, who are the strong players? And who are the weak ones? How do we keep track of them accurately and on a timely basis? In the stock market, the strong hands are the insiders; and the weak hands are the odd-lot buyers.

In the futures markets, the strong hands are the **commercials** or **hedgers,** those who buy and sell futures almost exclusively as a protection against price changes in the actual bonds, stocks, currencies or commodities which they own. The weak hands are the **speculators,** especially the **small speculators** who are in the market strictly to make a quick profit and are not involved in the business of producing, selling or buying the actual bonds, stocks or commodities.

Certainly there are some speculators who do extremely well in the markets, making substantial profits year after year. And, conversely, there are no doubt some commercials who often perform poorly. But when taken as a group, there can be absolutely no doubt about one thing: The commercials are usually the **winners** and the speculators are usually the losers. How do you know when a major move is about to begin? Very simple: You just look for a significant **imbalance** between them— *a visible departure from the normal trading pattern.*

A typical example is what happened to the price of oil in 1985. Throughout the summer, the press was full of news about the great world oil glut. Sheik Yamani of Saudi Arabia threatened daily to take "drastic action" to boost production.

But behind the scenes, where very few were looking, an important shift was taking place. Hoards of small speculators were going short crude oil, heating oil and other oil products. Meanwhile, a few big oil companies, with vast capital reserves to back them up, were buying heavily on a scale down. Soon oil prices began to move higher, and continued to march upward for most of the remainder of the year.

By the end of November, after prices had risen steadily for nearly five months, these positions had been reversed. Now it was the little guy who owned the oil and the big guy who was on the other side of the market. Sure enough, as soon as OPEC abandoned its pricing policy, there began one of the sharpest price declines in recent history. It proved that the small speculator had been right in the first place. Trouble is, his timing was lousy, and he failed to stick to his guns.

By combining our W.O.W. studies with Hadady's Bullish Consensus we have found that we can generate consistently accurate signals for timing most markets. But no method, however good in the present, will consistently work in the future. Not only is the structure of the market in a state of rapid flux, but the indicator or method itself, as it becomes more widely known, can gain or lose accuracy.

II

THE BASICS OF
TECHNICAL ANALYSIS

4

TECHNICAL ANALYSIS AND CHARTING

There are essentially two methods of investing or speculating in markets. You can use external or "fundamental" information such as the profit outlook of an individual company, overall economic forecasts or the potential supply and demand of a particular commodity.

Or you can use strictly internal or "technical" information which ignores the fundamentals and focuses instead upon the actual patterns in the price movements and the actual buying and selling in the marketplace. The advantages of the technical analysis are very clear:

(1) Unless you have a very sophisticated and accurate forecasting model (even the largest computer models in the world—at Brookings Institute, Chase Econometrics or the Federal Reserve Board—are notorious for their inaccuracies) or unless you subscribe to the newsletter of a very astute forecaster, by the time you receive the information, most other investors have also received it and have reacted accordingly, pushing the price up or down. In other words, the fundamental information is almost invariably *already* reflected in the market.

(2) There are so many contradictory fundamentals impacting the market at any one time and so many "structural changes" in how these fundamental factors interact that it is often impossible to know how to weigh them. Again, this process of evaluation is all done by the marketplace itself and reflected in the price.

(3) In addition,   your computer can readily zero in on technical analysis and make cold and unbiased judgments; whereas fundamental information would normally require much more extensive interpretation on your part.

When you stop and think about this, it will become clear. You can't possibly know more about the value of a company's stock than its own board of directors. Likewise, in the commodity markets, you will never know more about crop conditions or the supply and demand factors at work on a certain commodity than the actual professionals that work in that industry. Fortunately, however, you don't have to.

Hundreds of years of price charts have shown us one basic truth—*prices move in trends*. A trend indicates there exists an inequality between the forces of supply and demand. Such changes in the forces of supply and demand are usually readily identifiable by the action of the market itself as displayed in the prices. Certain patterns or formations which appear on the charts have a meaning and can be interpreted in terms of probable future trend development.

Charts are the working tools of the technical analyst. Until very recently, most charting was done manually. At best, you could subscribe to a chartmaking service (of which there are many excellent ones). They produce daily charts which are mailed to you weekly. You then put in the prices each day until your new chartbook arrives the following week—no problem as long as you are not trying to follow too many stocks and commodities. If you are, however, it could be quite a time consuming job. This is where a computer *would* come in handy.

If you own a computer, you have a further advantage in charting—flexibility. When you are dependent upon a chart service, you must see the market from the perspective which they arbitrarily select. Your computer, on the other hand, allows you to control the amount of history you wish to view. You may change the spacing between days. You may look at the data as daily, weekly or monthly. You have the ability to magnify selected portions of the chart. The following examples − representing the same general period for the Dow Jones Industrial Average—show how identical price patterns may be viewed through different perspectives using the graphical capabilities of your computer.

Figure 4-1 is a simple high-low chart packed tightly with *no* space between each day's price.

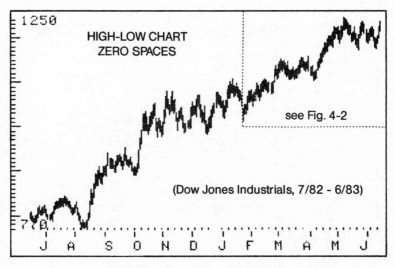

Figure 4-1

But notice in figure 4-2 how the pattern is clarified by adding one space between each day's price, although now only half of the time span fits on the page.

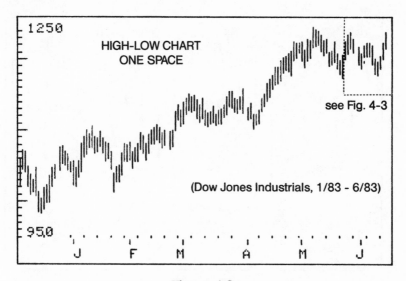

Figure 4-2

Figure 4-3 provides an entirely different perspective as nine spaces are added between each day's price.

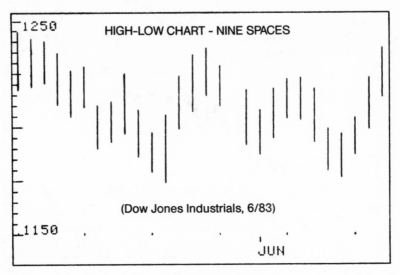

Figure 4-3

Figure 4-4 adds two additional elements of information—the opening and closing price for each day.

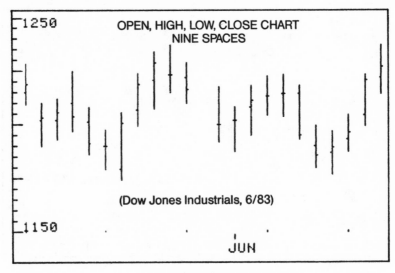

Figure 4-4

Figure 4-5 is a "close only" chart—one continuous line connecting each day's close. It is an extremely valuable analytical tool rarely offered by chart services.

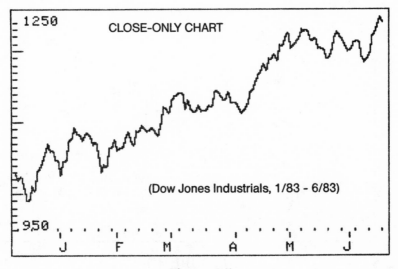

Figure 4-5

In figure 4-6, we adjust our scales so as to make the price pattern appear flatter, still another advantage of your computerized charting.

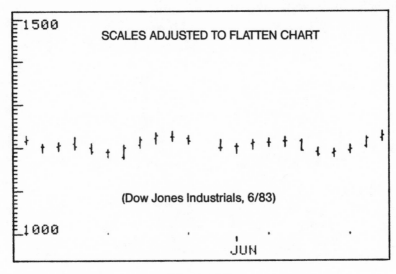

Figure 4-6

You can view a much broader time perspective in figure 4-7 which uses data in weekly—rather than daily—form.

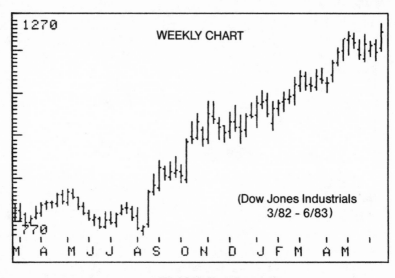

FIGURE 4-7

These are only a few of the myriad of possibilities. The charts themselves, however, are not the goal. Rather, they are simply a handy device for revealing to you—at a glance—critical trends and chart patterns which will help guide your investment decisions.

5

TRENDS AND TRENDLINES

Prices move in trends because of an imbalance between supply and demand. When the supply of a stock or commodity is greater than the demand, the trend will be down as there are more sellers than buyers; when demand exceeds supply, the trend will be up as buyers "bid up" the price; and if the forces of supply and demand are nearly equal, the market will move sideways in what is called a "trading range." Eventually, new information will enter the market and the market will begin to trend again either up or down, depending on whether the new information is taken as positive or negative.

Remember, you can profit in **both** an *uptrend* or a *downtrend* by *buying* or *selling short*—selling borrowed stocks which you hope to buy back later at a lower price. When you buy, it is said you are "going long" and you "are long" or "stay long" until you sell out. When you sell short, the expressions used are "go short," "be short" or "stay short." A major uptrend is a "bull market" and an opportunity to profit by being "bullish." A major downtrend is a "bear market" so you will want to stay "bearish." The key to trend analysis, of course, is to determine *when the pattern will change* so that you can shift in time from bearish to bullish or vice-versa.

Trends which are very brief are called *minor* trends; those lasting a few weeks are known as *intermediate* trends; and trends lasting for a period of months are *major* trends.

TRENDLINES will help you determine what trend is in force. If a market is moving up, you draw a line connecting each successively higher bottom. As long as the market remains on or above this line, the uptrend is in force. Conversely, in a downtrend, you would draw a line connecting each successively lower top. As long as prices remain on or below this line, the downtrend is in force:

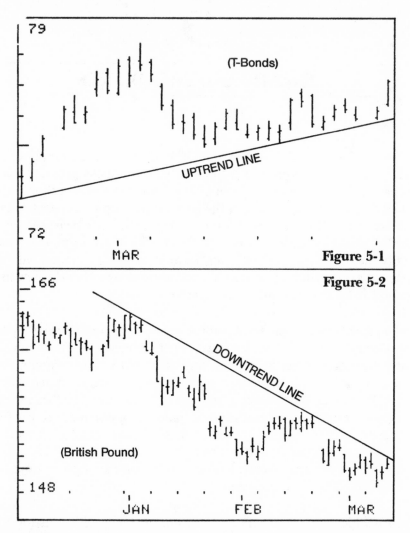

Figure 5-1

Figure 5-2

Trendline theory states that once a trendline is penetrated, the trend which was previously in force is reversed. Thus, if an uptrend line is penetrated, it is a signal to sell; and if a downtrend line is penetrated, it is a signal to buy. But there is still more to know about trendlines.

Let's say your downtrend line has just been decisively broken and you now believe we are starting a new uptrend. You can't draw a new uptrend line yet because you only have one bottom. You must wait until prices move higher for about a week, then react downward for a couple of days, and later start moving higher again. This will give you a second, somewhat higher bottom which you can connect to the first bottom to form an uptrend line. So far, so good.

If prices, after moving higher, react downward and form a third bottom on the trendline, the trendline then becomes more valid. We say that prices "tested" the trendline and it "held." The longer this trendline remains intact, the more authority it will have.

You will find that very steep trendlines are not very authoritative in that they will often be broken by a brief sideways movement or "consolidation," after which prices shoot up again. It is the trendlines with the gentler slope—either upward or downward—that usually offer more technical significance.

In sum, factors to consider in weighing the validity of a trendline include: (a) number of bottoms (or tops) that have formed on or near the trendline, (b) the overall duration of the trendline and (c) the steepness of the angle.

Getting back to our example, what if the market accelerates and a third bottom is formed way above our trendline? Now where is the real trend?

We may have to wait until the fourth bottom forms before we know for sure. Until then, it would be a good idea to draw in two trendlines, A and B:

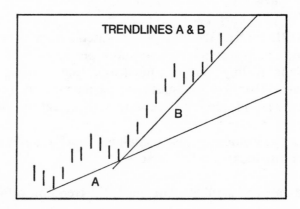

Figure 5-3

FAN LINES. When a market drops sharply, you will of course have a steep downtrend line. Often this trendline will be broken by a sharp rally, at which point a new trendline must be drawn. At a later date, this second trendline might be broken by a rally and a third trendline would need to be drawn. Such lines are known as "fan lines."

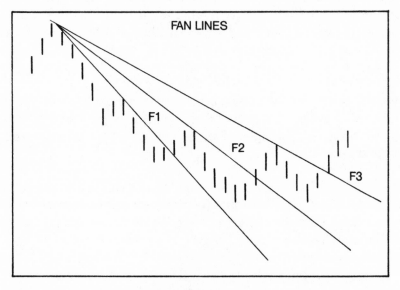

Figure 5-4

The rule is that when the third fan line has been broken, the trend has changed to the upside. In rising markets, this rule can also be applied in reverse.

VALID PENETRATIONS. As stated earlier, a penetration of an up-trend line is a signal to sell; and a penetration of a downtrend line is a signal to buy. But let's not forget that charting is an art and not a science. Therefore, we must appraise the validity of the penetration. Here are a few questions to ask when a penetration occurs:

Was penetration by just a small amount? If so, it remains suspect and we must look at other factors.

Did the price actually *close* below the trendline or was it merely the low of the day which broke the trend, an event which we call penetration on an "intraday basis"? An intraday break often is not sufficient evidence to confirm a change in trend; and even the close itself should be *significantly* below the trendline.

Did *volume* pick up on the day in question? If so, there is a good chance the trendline break was valid. Was the break accompanied by a gap or a reversal pattern? (Gaps and reversal patterns are discussed in Chapters 7 and 9.) If so, this would also lend credence to a change in trend.

Conversely, did the penetration occur as a result of several days of sideways movement? This would look more like a test of the trendline than a penetration of it. Further movement up or down should be awaited before a conclusion is drawn.

"PULLBACKS" or "throwbacks" are very interesting phenomena that often occur after the breaking of a trendline. Here's what happens in this case: An uptrend line is broken. Prices continue lower for a few days. Then they rally back right up to the trendline again. Finally, the market proceeds to move lower. (The reverse would occur upon the breaking of a downtrend line.)

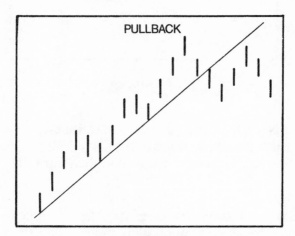

Figure 5-5

In the example illustrated in figure 5-5, you can see that the pullback actually caused prices to go higher than the price at which the trendline was broken. Thus, had you sold short when the trendline was broken, you would have a loss a few days later. One way many professionals handle this situation is to wait for the pullback before selling short. One problem here is that sometimes the pullback never materializes and you wind up selling short at much lower levels or missing the move completely. I usually recommend selling half of your positions on the trendline break and the other half on the pullback.

TREND CHANNELS. In an uptrend, you can construct a trend channel by drawing a line *parallel* to the uptrend line using as your starting point an intermediate top made between two successively higher bottoms:

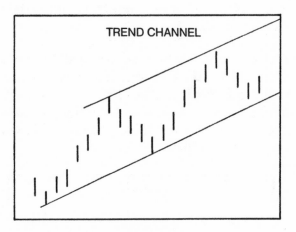

Figure 5-6

RETURN LINE. This second line is often called the "return line" since it marks the area where reaction against the prevailing trend originates. The area between the basic trendline and the return line is the "trend channel."

This return line is less reliable than the basic trendline but is valuable enough to be considered in your trading strategy. One short-term trading strategy applied by professionals in an up market is to buy on or near the basic trendline and take profits on or near the return line. Another variation on this technique is to draw a parallel line equidistant between the basic trendline and return line. Now you have an upper channel or "sell zone," and a lower channel or "buy zone" (Figure 5-7).

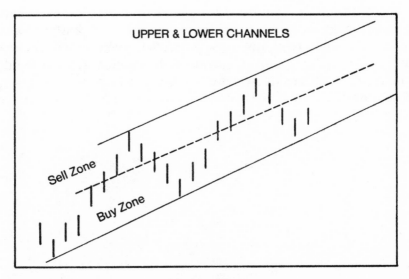

Figure 5-7

A return line can also be used to forewarn of an impending change in trend. Any time prices fail to move up to the area of the return line, you can consider the market is weakening. Use this as a warning and be on the alert for a break of the trendline the next time prices approach it:

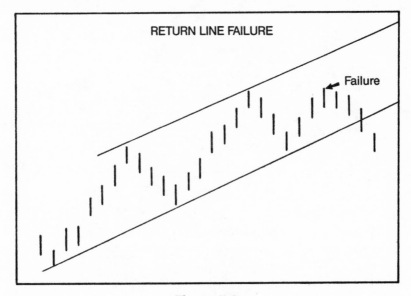

Figure 5-8

The main problem with trendline analysis is that it's too easy and, as a result, many an investor and trader can follow it, pushing prices up or down prematurely, making it difficult for you to make *your* trade in time to catch the move. Therefore, in Chapter 7, we delve deeper into chart analysis to find ways of *predicting* a break in a trend—*before* it becomes obvious to the average investor. But first let's examine one more critical factor—volume.

6

VOLUME

In the stock market, volume refers to the number of shares that change hands on a given day. In commodity markets, it refers to the number of contracts traded. Each transaction is the result of the meeting of demand, on the one hand, with supply on the other. When demand exceeds supply, prices tend to rise. Conversely, when supply exceeds demand, prices tend to fall. Therefore, volume occurring during advances is termed "demand volume"; volume occurring during declines is "supply volume."

We study volume because it can be a measure of supply and demand. There are many ways to visualize the relationship of volume and prices. Some analysts think of volume as a gauge of market pressure. Our own particular "picture" is this: Imagine you have turned on the garden hose and are pointing it skyward. You toss a plastic ball into the stream of water, and it shoots upward. But if you turn down the water pressure, what happens to the ball? It continues upward from its own momentum for a second or two, but then falls back. It can't continue higher until you increase the water pressure. Like the plastic ball, prices need increasing volume to continue higher. When prices move higher, but on diminished volume, they are likely to fall back.

The basic rules of volume analysis are as follows:

1. When prices are rising and volume is increasing, the present trend will continue, i.e., prices will continue to rise.

2. When prices are rising and volume is decreasing, the present trend is not likely to continue, i.e.,the price rise will decelerate and then turn downward.

3. When prices are falling and volume is increasing, the present trend will continue, i.e., prices will continue to fall.

4. When prices are falling and volume is decreasing, the present trend is not likely to continue, i.e., the price decline will decelerate and then prices will turn upward.

5. When volume is not rising or falling, the effect on price is neutral.

How can technical analysis employ this concept in practical applications? Let's assume XYZ stock has been in a trading range for several weeks with an average daily volume of 50,000 shares changing hands. Prices now begin to move higher and the daily volume picks up to 80,000 shares. We are justified in believing that prices will continue higher, fueled by "demand volume." Sure enough, prices do continue to move higher on strong volume over the next three weeks.

Then, in the fourth week, prices tumble and lose 30% of their previous gains. Do we sell the stock or hold? Again, the clue lies in the volume picture. We notice that during the fallback, XYZ stock has been trading only 40,000 shares per day. Therefore using our volume rules, we can surmise that this is only a *temporary* reaction. What might be actually happening in the marketplace? Any number of factors could be contributing to the fall in prices. Early buyers could be taking profits or any new buyers could be waiting for a setback before buying. All of these are natural, healthy reasons for a correction and, therefore, we have no reason to abandon our position at this point...unless we notice that volume is beginning to increase on down days.

As expected, in week 5, prices begin shooting up again on volume averaging 90,000 shares a day. Week 6 continues in the same way. Week 7 brings a reaction in prices, but again on reduced volume of 50,000 shares per day. We hold our stock. Week 8 sees prices rising again to new highs, but volume—oddly enough—is only averaging 60,000 shares per day. This is a clear-cut warning signal: Demand volume is drying up. New demand may still come into the market if favorable news events occur, but if not, prices are in danger. Remember, prices can only go up if fueled by rising demand volume, but if they fail to get that extra boost, they can fall under their own weight. As expected, prices turn down the next few days on heavy volume; we sell our stock.

The XYZ example represents only one possible scenario. What if prices have been in a sideways trading range and then begin to fall on low volume. Would we consider this move false? Not necessarily. Although prices must be accompanied by strong volume to confirm an up move, *down* moves often begin on light volume. Remember, a market can fall under its own weight; and it is important to be aware that *volume usually tends to be lighter when prices are falling than when rising*.

In the XYZ example, the last phase or "leg" of the move was on light volume. But oddly enough, tops may also be formed on *heavy* volume—a "climax" which usually occurs after a market has been moving up for a considerable amount of time.

This is a contradiction which reflects a classical problem which has puzzled technical analysts for many years and there is no complete solution. However, if you closely observe the market action it may help you determine if it is a climax or not. Typically, prices make new highs in the morning on heavy volume, but by afternoon, prices are substantially lower while volume is still heavy, producing a reversal day (see Chapter 7). This is a classic example of "distribution'—a period when previous owners of the stock are dumping their shares and taking profits, while Johnny-Come-Latelies are buying it at the top. The previous owners who have been buying for weeks have more stock to distribute than the Latelies can handle. So, supply overcomes demand, prices crash, and the new buyers are left holding the bag. Stocks are said to be "moving from strong hands to weak hands."

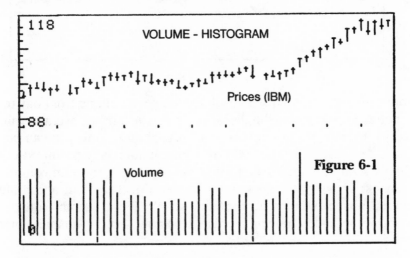

Figure 6-1

Bottoms often display quite the opposite pattern, occurring on light volume. Volume tends to dry up, indicating a lessening of supply pressure. If prices then move higher on increased volume, it is a good sign that the decline has ended.

How do we graphically represent volume? The traditional way has been in the form of a bar chart directly beneath the price chart (Figure 6-1).

However, you need not be so limited. You can also look at volume in many different ways. When looking at the actual volume itself, I prefer to chart it as a continuous line, rather than a bar chart. Notice also, I leave more space between each day's price so I can readily identify the corresponding change in volume for *each* day:

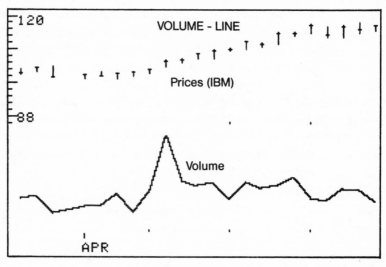

Figure 6-2

Some analysts feel that the absolute change in volume from day to day is not as important as the deviation from the current average volume. Again, by using your computer as an analytical tool, you can be way ahead of those who must rely only on commercially produced charts. Here's what you do: First, run a 10-day moving average on volume (for more on moving averages, see Chapter 13). Then run a continuous line of current volume on the same graph. If the current volume line is above the 10-day moving average, we know that the volume is increasing. Conversely, when the current volume is below the 10-day moving average, volume is decreasing:

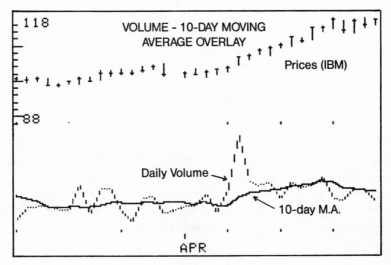

Figure 6-3

In sum, an understanding of volume patterns adds a third dimension to our analysis. Now we're ready to begin to apply these concepts to key patterns which appear on our charts.

7

REVERSAL PATTERNS

In Chapter 5, we noted that one way to tell if a trend has changed is to watch for a breaking of the trendline; and in Chapter 6 we saw how volume patterns may or may not confirm this change. Further investigation would show us that when a price trend is in the process of reversal—either from up to down or from down to up—a *characteristic pattern* takes shape on the chart and becomes recognizable as a "reversal formation."

THE HEAD AND SHOULDERS TOP formation is one of the most common and also one of the most reliable of all the major reversal patterns.

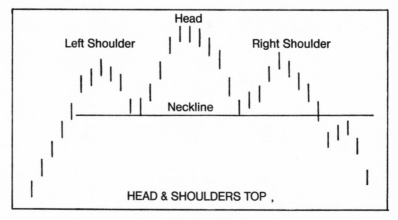

Figure 7-1

It consists of a left shoulder, a head and a right shoulder.

The left shoulder is formed usually at the end of an extensive advance during which volume is quite heavy. At the end of the left shoulder, there is usually a small dip or recession which typically occurs on low volume.

The head then forms with heavy volume on the upside and with lesser volume accompanying the subsequent reaction. At this point, in order to conform to proper form, prices must come down somewhere *near* the low of the left shoulder—somewhat lower perhaps or somewhat higher but, in any case, below the top of the left shoulder.

The right shoulder is then formed by a rally on usually less volume than any previous rallies in this formation.

A neckline can now be drawn across the bottoms of the left shoulder, the head and right shoulder. A breaking of this neckline on a decline from the right shoulder is the final confirmation and completes the Head and Shoulders Top formation. This is, therefore, your signal to sell short.

A word of caution. Very often, after moving lower, prices will pull back to the neckline before continuing their descent. You may wait for this pullback to sell or use it as a point to add to your original short positions.

Most Head and Shoulders are not perfectly symmetrical. One shoulder may appear to droop. Also, the time involved in the development of each shoulder may vary, causing the structure to lose symmetry. The neckline, rather than being horizontal, may be sloping up or down. The only qualification on an up-sloping neckline is that the lowest point on the right shoulder must be appreciably lower than that of the top of the left shoulder.

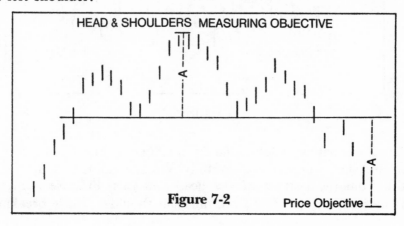

HEAD & SHOULDERS MEASURING OBJECTIVE

Figure 7-2

Price Objective

A Head and Shoulders formation can also be extremely useful in estimating the probable extent of the move once the neckline has been penetrated.

Here's what you do: Referring to figure 7-2, measure the distance vertically from the top of the head to the neckline. Then measure the same distance down from the point where prices penetrated the neckline (following the completion of the right shoulder). This gives you the minimum objective of how far prices should decline following the successful completion of the Head and Shoulders Top. To double check your estimate, one guideline to look at is the extent of the previous rise. If the up move preceding the Head and Shoulders Top has been small, the ensuing down move may be small as well. Thus, the extent of the previous advance should be at least as large as the objective you have estimated from the formation.

THE HEAD AND SHOULDERS BOTTOM formation is simply the inverse of a Head and Shoulders Top, and often indicates a trend reversal from down to up. The typical Head and Shoulders Bottom formation is illustrated in figure 7-3.

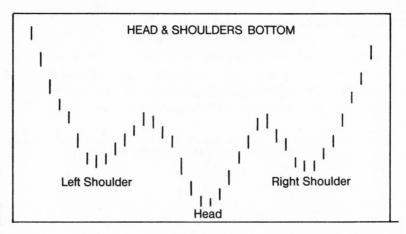

Figure 7-3

The volume pattern is somewhat different in a Head and Shoulders Bottom and should be watched carefully. Volume should pick up as prices rally from the bottom of the head and then increase even more dramatically on the rally from the right shoulder. If the breaking of

the neckline is done on low volume we must be suspect of this formation. The breakout could be false, only to be followed by a retest of
the lows. A high volume breakout, on the other hand, would give us
good reason to believe the Head and Shoulders Bottom formation is
genuine.

The only other noticeable difference in the Head and Shoulders Bottom formation is that it may sometimes appear flatter than the Head
and Shoulder Top. Often the turns are more rounded. Otherwise, all
the rules and measuring objectives can be applied equally well.

DOUBLE TOP FORMATIONS appear as an "M" on a chart as in
figure 7-4. They are very "popular." But watch out! Many analysts often
mislabel and misinterpret Double Top and Bottom formations. In any
uptrend, after a reaction, each new wave up will appear to be "making" a Double Top (see figure 7-5).

But in truth, at this point there is *absolutely no evidence pointing to*

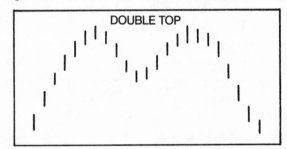

Figure 7-4

a Double Top. Nine times out of ten, the trend will remain in force and
prices will simply go on to make new highs. So don't be fooled. You
have no confirmation whatsoever of a Double Top until the valley has
been broken as in figure 7-6.

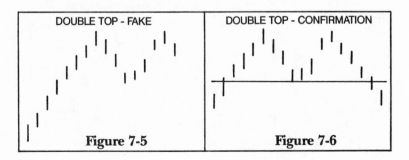

Figure 7-5   **Figure 7-6**

Volume, again, can offer a clue in the formation of this pattern. If the volume on the rise of the second peak is less than on the first peak, you have an initial indication that prices may fail to go above the previous high, turn around and go on to confirm the double Top. High volume accompanying the second rise would minimize that possibility.

Another factor to use in determining the validity of a Double Top formation is the time element. If two tops appear at the same level but quite close together in time, the chances are good that they are merely part of a consolidation area. If, on the other hand, the peaks are separated by a deep and long reaction, this is more likely a true Double Top:

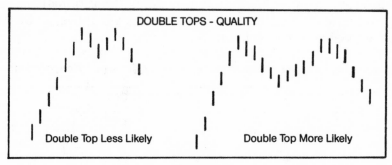

Figure 7-7

As with the Head and Shoulders formation, a pullback to the valley area is very possible. If you wish to measure the objective from the breakout point, you can simply take the distance from peak to valley and subtract from the valley to the "M" as in figure 7-8.

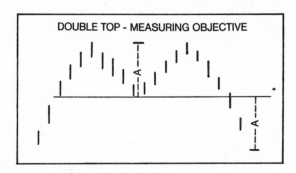

Figure 7-8

DOUBLE BOTTOMS are the inverse of Double Tops and appear on the charts as a W formation:

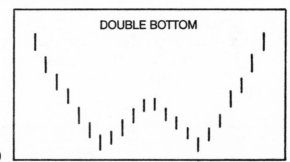

Figure 7-9

All of the rules associated with Double Top formations also apply to Double Bottoms. The volume patterns, of course, are different. A valid Double Bottom should show a marked increase in volume on the rally up from the second bottom.

TRIPLE TOPS are more rare than Double Tops. They appear on a chart similar to the pattern shown in figure 7-10.

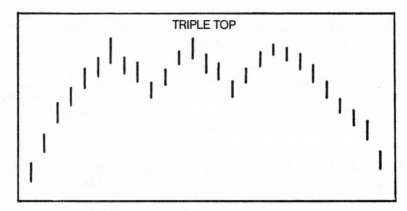

Figure 7-10

Volume is usually less on the second advance, and still less on the third. The highs need not be spaced as far apart as those which constitute a Double Top, and they need not be equally spaced. Also, the intervening valleys need not bottom out at exactly the same level; either the first or the second may be deeper. But the triple top is not confirmed until prices have broken through both valleys.

There are several different trading strategies that can be employed to take advantage of the Triple Top formation. After a Double Top has been confirmed, if prices are rallying again but on light volume, it is a good place to sell short with a stop (exit point) above the highest peak of the Double Top:

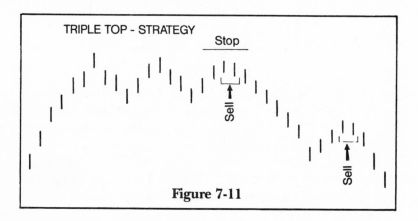

Figure 7-11

Another good place to sell would be after a Triple Top has formed and a fourth lower top is being formed.

If, however, prices continue to rally up to the level of the three previous peaks, they usually go higher; and if prices descend to the same level a fourth time, they usually go lower. It is very rare to see four tops or bottoms at equal levels.

TRIPLE BOTTOMS are simply Triple Tops turned upside down and all the rules can be applied in reverse. (Figure 7-12).

The accompanying volume pattern, however, is different. The third low should be on light volume and the ensuing rally from that bottom should show a considerable pickup in activity.

ROUNDING TOPS AND BOTTOMS. Because Rounding Tops are so rare, we will limit our discussion to Rounding Bottoms, commonly referred to as "Saucer Bottoms."

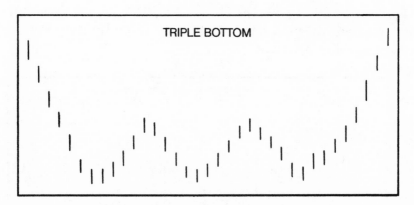

Figure 7-12

The chart pattern in figure 7-13 shows a gradual change in the trend direction, produced by a step-by-step shift in the balance of power between buying and selling. As we begin a Rounded Bottom, we will notice volume decreasing as selling pressure eases. The trend then becomes neutral with very little trading activity occurring. As prices start up, volume increases as well. Finally, price and volume continue to accelerate, with prices often literally blasting out of this pattern.

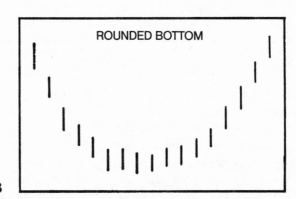

Figure 7-13

BROADENING FORMATIONS, such as the one illustrated in figure 7-14, usually have bearish implications. They appear much more frequently at tops than at bottoms and, for that reason, we will limit our discussion to Broadening Tops. The theory is that *five minor reversals are followed by a substantial decline.* In the classic pattern, reversals #3 and #5 occur at successively higher points than reversal #1; and reversal

#4 occurs at a lower point than reversal #2. This same characteristic pattern was evident on many individual stocks in the third quarter of 1929, preceding the great crash.

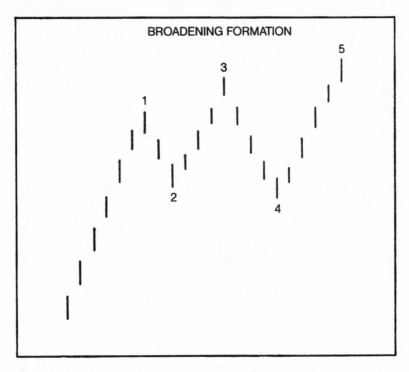

Figure 7-14

The Broadening Top formation usually suggests a market that is lacking support from the "smart money" and is out of control. Quite often, well informed selling is completed during the early stages of the formation; and in the later stages, the participation is from the less informed, more excitable public. Volume is often very irregular and offers no clue as to the direction of the subsequent breakout. The price swings themselves are very unpredictable so it is difficult to tell where each swing will end.

Broadening Tops are a difficult formation to trade. However, you can usually be quite sure the trend has turned down after a break of the lower of the two valleys.

WEDGE FORMATIONS. Up until now, the reversal formations we have discussed have all been powerful enough to reverse an intermediate or major trend. The Wedges, on the other hand, usually only reverse a *minor* trend and, as a general rule of thumb, should typically take 3 weeks or so to complete. It is a chart formation in which price fluctuations are confined within converging straight lines. These form a pattern which itself may have a rising or falling slant.

In a **RISING WEDGE**, both boundary lines slant up from left to right but the lower line rises at a steeper angle than the upper line. After breaking the lower line boundary, prices usually decline in earnest:

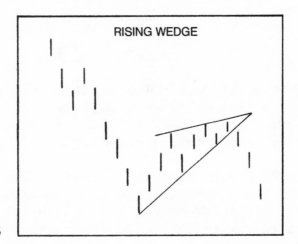

Figure 7-15

Generally, each new price advance, or wave up, is feebler than the last, indicating that investment demand is weakening at the higher price levels. Rising Wedges are usually more reliable when found in a Bear Market. In a Bull Market, what appears to be a Rising Wedge may actually be a continuation pattern known as a "Flag" or "Pennant" (discussed in the next chapter). This is more likely to be true if the Wedge is less than three weeks in length.

In a **FALLING WEDGE**, both boundary lines slant down from right to left but the upper line descends at a steeper angle than the lower line. Differing from the Rising Wedge, once prices move out of a Falling Wedge, they are more apt to drift sidewise and "saucer-out" before beginning to rise. (Figure 7-16).

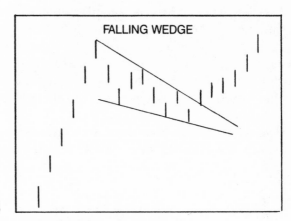

Figure 7-16

Minor Reversal Patterns

A REVERSAL DAY TOP occurs when prices move higher but then close near the lows of the day, usually below their opening and below the mid-point of the day's range. An even stronger reversal is indicated if the close is below the previous day's close. (Figure 7-17).

A REVERSAL DAY BOTTOM occurs when prices move lower but then close near the highs of the day, usually above the opening and above the mid-point of the day's range. An even stronger reversal is indicated if the close is above the previous day's close. (Figure 7-18).

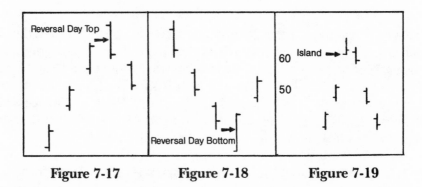

Figure 7-17　　　　**Figure 7-18**　　　　**Figure 7-19**

THE ISLAND REVERSAL. Suppose the price of a stock in a rising market closes at its high of 50 and then on the following day, opens at its low of 60, leaving a "gap" of 10 points (see chapter nine). A few days later, the market moves back down and forms another gap in approximately the same 50-60 area. Thus, all the trading above 60 will appear on the chart to be *isolated*, like an island, from all previous and subsequent fluctuations. This is called an "island reversal."

Island Reversals are quite rare, but are an extremely good indicator of a reversal in the trend. Their appearance indicates that an extreme change in sentiment has occurred.

Thus, we have seen various patterns which can often signal a critical change in market direction. In the chapter to follow, you will see various formations which give you precisely the opposite indication. We recommend you compare these chapters carefully and bear in mind the key differences between these formations whenever making a trading decision.

8

CONSOLIDATION PATTERNS

We have seen how trends are reversed. But at other times, a trend may be interrupted, resulting in sideways movement for a time, before continuing on in its previous direction. Such sideways movements may even result in a break of the trendline. These formations are known as "consolidation" or "continuation patterns." The ability to differentiate between reversal patterns and continuation patterns is vital.

TRIANGLES have occasionally been known to reverse a trend. But usually they act as a period of consolidation from which prices continue on in the same direction. Triangles form as a result of indecision on the part of both buyers and sellers. During this time, market participants tend to withdraw to the sidelines, resulting in narrower market fluctuations and diminishing volume. A breakout of the triangle usually occurs as the result of some news affecting the market. And this breakout, if legitimate, is accompanied by a sharp increase in volume.

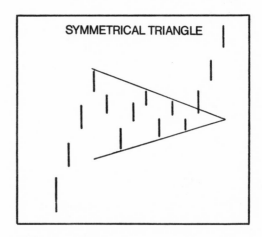

Figure 8-1

THE SYMMETRICAL TRIANGLE , sometimes known as a "coil," is the most common type. It is formed by a succession of price fluctuations, each of which is smaller than its predecessor, resulting in a pattern bounded by a downslanting line and an upslanting line. (Figure 8-1).

A Symmetrical Triangle, by definition, must have at least four reversal points. From that point onward, the breakout may occur at any time in the triangle, even before reaching its apex. More powerful moves are found when prices break out decisively at a point somewhere between half and three-quarters of the distance between the left side of the triangle and the apex.

Symmetrical Triangles are not as reliable as the Head and Shoulders formations, and really work out only about two-thirds of the time because they are subject to false breakouts called "End Runs" or "Shakeouts":

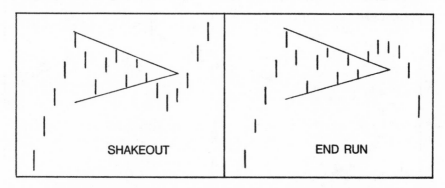

| Figure 8-2 | Figure 8-3 |

There is no way to avoid getting caught in such false moves—unless you recognize their characteristic volume patterns. A breakout to the upside should be on high volume. If volume is light, be suspect of a possible false move and "End Run."

Downside breakouts are a different matter. Prices often break out on low volume with a pickup in volume not occurring for a few days. Oddly enough, a high-volume breakout on the downside is often the signal of a "Shakeout."

RIGHT-ANGLE TRIANGLES, both Ascending and Descending, are better predictors of the future direction of prices than Symmetrical Triangles. In theory, prices will break toward the flat side—upward in an Ascending Triangle and downward in a Descending Triangle.

THE ASCENDING RIGHT-ANGLE TRIANGLE is characterized by a top-line boundary that is horizontal and a bottom-line that is sloping upward. (Figure 8-4).

This formation occurs when demand is growing yet continues to meet supply at a fixed price. If demand continues, the supply being distributed at that price will eventually be entirely absorbed by new buyers, and prices will then advance rapidly.

THE DESCENDING RIGHT-ANGLE TRIANGLE will exhibit a horizontal lower boundary and a down-sloping upper boundary:

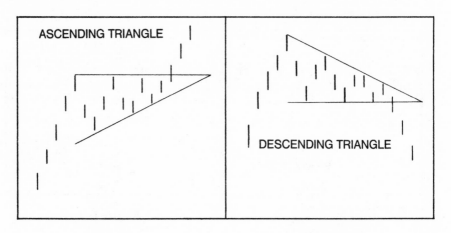

ASCENDING TRIANGLE

DESCENDING TRIANGLE

Figure 8-4   **Figure 8-5**

This formation occurs when there is a certain amount of demand at a fixed price yet supply continues to come into the market. Eventually, the demand is exhausted and prices break out of the triangle on the downside.

Triangles, both Symmetrical and Right-Angle, can be used for some measuring though they are not as reliable as the Head-and-Shoulders measuring formula. Assuming, for example, a breakout on the upside, you simply draw a line parallel to the lower side of the triangle and expect prices to rally up to that line:

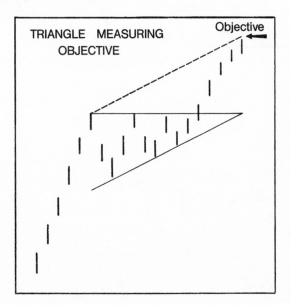

Figure 8-6

Also, prices should resume their uptrend at the same approximate angle as the uptrend which preceded the triangle's formation.

THE RECTANGLE formation, sometimes known as a "line," forms as a result of a battle between two groups of approximately equal strength. Although offering little forecasting ability as to which direction the breakout should occur, once prices begin to move out of the formation, it can be very useful in setting objectives. (Figure 8-7).

Volume characteristics are similar to triangles in that volume tends to diminish as the Rectangle lengthens. Breakouts have less tendency to be false than with the Symmetrical Triangles. However, breakouts are more likely to be followed by a pullback.

All in all, there is a somewhat greater tendency for Rectangles to be consolidation rather than reversal patterns. When a Rectangle is a reversal pattern, it is much more likely to occur at a major or intermediate bottom rather than at a top.

A minimum measuring objective can be derived from adding the width of the Rectangle to the point of breakout. Normally, wide-swinging Rectangles will offer more dynamic moves than the narrower ones. A move out of a narrow Rectangle will often hesitate at its minimum objective before moving on:

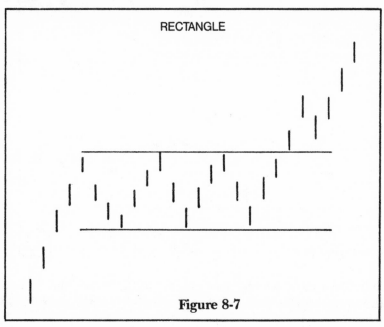

RECTANGLE

Figure 8-7

FLAGS AND PENNANTS are true consolidation patterns and are very reliable indicators both in terms of direction and measuring. In an up

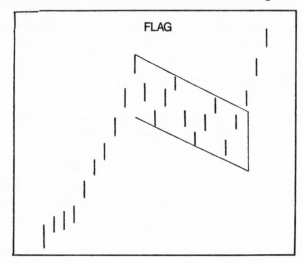

FLAG

Figure 8-8

market, flags usually form after a dynamic, nearly straight move up on heavy volume. Prices react on lower volume and a series of minor fluctuations eventually form a downward-sloping, compact parallelogram. (Figure 8-8).

The pennant is very similar to the flag except that it is bounded by converging rather than parallel lines:

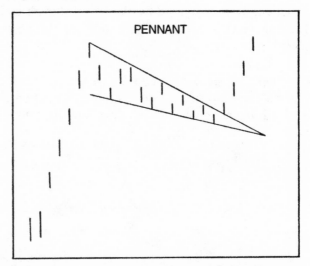

Figure 8-9

Flags and pennants, in order to be considered valid should conform to three rules—(1) they should occur after a very sharp up or down move;

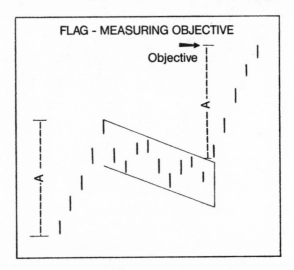

Figure 8-10

(2) volume should decline throughout the duration of the pattern; and (3) prices should break out of the pattern within a matter of a few weeks.

The measuring formula for flags and pennants is identical. You simply add the height of the "pole," formed in the move preceding the formation, to the breakout point of the flag. (Figure 8-10).

In practice, price may tend to overshoot this objective somewhat in an advancing market, while falling short of the objective in a declining market.

All of these patterns help confirm a trend. But looking more closely at market fluctuations, we notice another phenomenon which can also give us additional clues—gaps. This is the subject of our next chapter.

9

GAPS

Gaps represent an area on the chart where no trading takes place. For example, if a stock reaches a high of, say, 50 on Monday, but then opens at 60 on Tuesday, moving straight up from the opening, no trading occurs in the 50-60 area. This no-trading zone appears on the chart as a hole or a "gap." Thus, in an uptrending market, a gap is produced when the highest price of any one day is lower than the lowest price of the following day, or the reverse in a downtrending market.

Gaps can be valuable in spotting the beginning of a move, measuring the extent of a move or confirming the end of a move. There are four different types of gaps: "Common gaps," "breakaway gaps," "measuring gaps," and "exhaustion gaps." Since each has its own distinctive implications, it is important to be able to distinguish between them.

COMMON GAPS—also known as "temporary gaps," "pattern gaps" or "area gaps"—tend to occur in a sideways trading range or price congestion area. Usually, the price moves back up or down subsequently as the market returns to the gap area in order to "fill the gap." If this does occur, the gap offers little in the way of forecasting significance.

It may be noted, however, that common gaps are more apt to develop in consolidation rather than in reversal formations. In other words, the appearance of many gaps within consolidation patterns (such as a Rectangle or Symmetrical Triangle) is a signal that the breakout should be in the same direction as that of the preceding trend. (Figure 9-1).

THE BREAKAWAY GAP occurs as prices break away from an area of congestion. Typically, prices will break away from an Ascending or Descending Triangle with a gap.

This gap implies that the change in sentiment has been strong and that the ensuing move will be powerful. Often the market does not return to "fill the gap," particularly if volume is heavy after the gap has formed. If volume is not heavy, there is a reasonable chance the gap will be filled before prices resume their trend. (Figure 9-2).

THE MEASURING GAP typically occurs in the middle of a price move and can be used to measure how much farther a move will go. Rather than being associated with a congestion area, it is more likely to occur in the course of a rapid, straight-line advance or decline, usually pat approximately the halfway point. (Figure 9-3).

THE EXHAUSTION GAP signals the end of a move. Like Measuring gaps, Exhaustion gaps are associated with rapid, extensive advances or declines. The problem, of course, is: how do you know whether it's a Measuring gap or an Exhaustion gap? One clue may be found in the volume. An Exhaustion gap is often accompanied by particularly high volume. Another method for detecting an Exhaustion Gap is with a Reversal Day. (Figure 9-4).

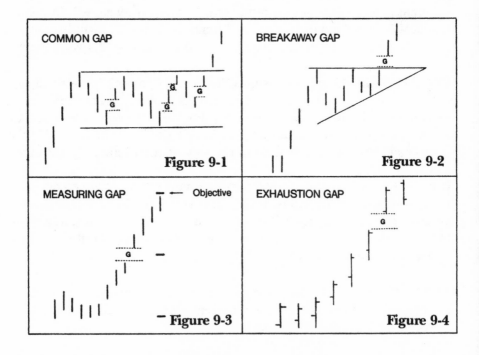

COMMON GAP

Figure 9-1

BREAKAWAY GAP

Figure 9-2

MEASURING GAP — Objective

Figure 9-3

EXHAUSTION GAP

Figure 9-4

Now, combining the concepts of the past several chapters, we have numerous tools for deciding when a market could be turning. The next question which arises is: How far will it go? Chapter 10 begins to provide some answers.

10

RETRACEMENT THEORY

No market moves steadily down or steadily up. Instead, each movement in the primary direction is followed by a reaction, which can, in turn, be followed by another thrust.

Each thrust, measured from bottom to top or top to bottom, is known as the "swing" or "move." Each reaction or rally retraces part of the move and, therefore, is known as a "retracement." When the reaction is greater than the move, we must consider that the trend has changed, at least, for the near term. Retracement theory sets predetermined target levels for these moves and lends itself readily to computer applications.

Of course, our first problem is to determine the primary trend. But once we are reasonably assured that the market is in a downtrend or an uptrend, the key is to know how far a move is likely to be retraced before the market resumes that trend. Knowing that, we could better judge an appropriate point to enter the market on a reaction. Aside from correctly judging the primary trend, correctly timing entries on reactions is probably the most important aspect of trading.

What is a "normal" retracement? This question has been debated for years. The general consensus is that a normal retracement recaptures between one-third and two-thirds of the previous move. Another school of thought says 40-60%. Most agree that the 50% retracement is the most likely.

W. D. Gann went as far as to divide each move into eighths and thirds, giving us 1/8, 1/4, 3/8, 1/3, 1/2, 5/8, 2/3, 3/4 and 7/8 as all possible retracement levels. Of these, the most important to him were the 1/2, 5/8, 3/4 and 7/8 levels. Meanwhile, students of Elliott Wave Theory consider the Fibonacci retracement levels of .382 and .618 to be the most critical. Our own work shows special significance attached to these numbers, especially the .618; and often we've seen markets react exactly to this level before moving on.

Therefore, on your charts, it would be a good idea to keep track of some of the significant retracement levels such as in figure 10-1.

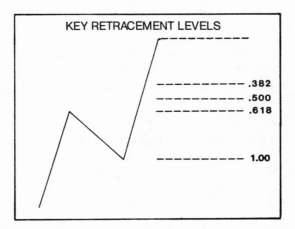

Figure 10-1

Keep in mind that each "move" is part of a larger move that has its own individual probable retracement levels. Consequently, you may want to go back and look at the current entire pattern in an even broader, longer-term perspective, viewing it as merely a retracement within the context of an even larger move.

Oft times, you will often find key retracement levels of different moves coinciding with one another, lending more credibility to your forecast that the market will indeed find support at that level.

11

SUPPORT AND RESISTANCE

In addition to retracement theory, what are some other ways of judging when a reaction or a rally is coming to an end and when the primary trend should resume? Support and resistance will give you some clues.

A SUPPORT LEVEL is a price level at which sufficient demand exists to at least temporarily halt a downward movement in prices.

A RESISTANCE LEVEL is a price at which sufficient supply exists to at least temporarily halt an upward movement.

In an uptrend, each former top—once surpassed—becomes a support level. In a downtrend, each former bottom—once penetrated—becomes a resistance level:

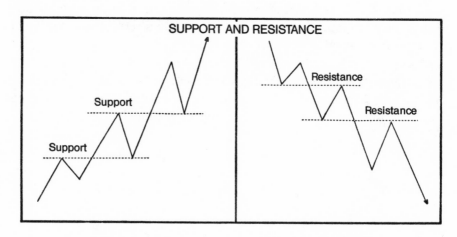

SUPPORT AND RESISTANCE

Support

Support

Resistance

Resistance

Figure 11-1   Figure 11-2

A congestion pattern forms an even more formidable support or resistance barrier since more actual trading took place at that price level:

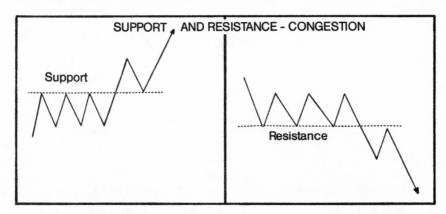

| Figure 11-3 | Figure 11-4 |

One more rule to remember: When a support level is broken, it becomes resistance, and when a resistance level is broken, it becomes support. How does this happen?

Let's take the hypothetical situation illustrated in figure 11-5. A group of buyers has been waiting on the sidelines and watching a stock decline from 80 to 60. At this price, they believe the stock is cheap so they buy. The stock begins to rise and eventually reaches 70. But they are confident the stock will go much higher. Unfortunately, the stock begins to decline and eventually falls to 50. At this point, the investors begin to feel they have made a mistake and vow to dump the stock if they can at least get their money back. Luckily, the stock begins to rally and as it reaches 60, these investors sell their shares, turning the stock price down once again.

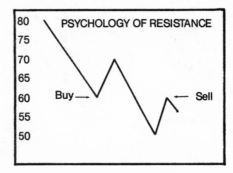

Figure 11-5

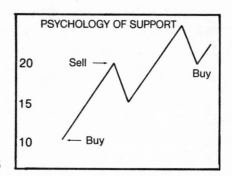

Figure 11-6

Months pass. Our same group of investors finds a hot new stock—ABC Company. (Refer to figure 11-6.) They buy it at 10 and, after a few months, the stock has risen to 20. This time they don't repeat the same mistake they made earlier. Instead, they sell the stock and pocket a huge profit. Two weeks later, the stock has dropped to 15 and they congratulate themselves for having taken their profits at 20. But a month later, the price of ABC has risen to 25. Now they don't feel so smart. "Maybe we should have held on longer for even more profit," is their refrain. They decide that if they get another chance to buy the stock again at 20, they will. This is one example of how previous tops can act as support.

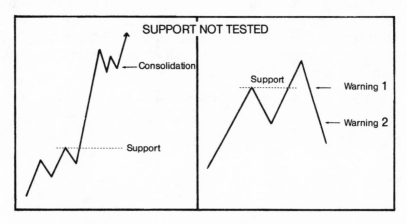

Figure 11-7   **Figure 11-8**

In figure 11-1, we showed a typical zigzag type of market, i.e., where each reaction found support at the previous top. Referring to figures 11-7 and 11-8, there are two other possibilities that can come up. A market may surge wildly, in which case we would not expect a reaction to take prices back to the previous top. Instead, on reaction, prices are likely to form a consolidation or reversal pattern somewhat above the price level of the previous top.

Another possibility is that prices break below their previous top, giving you your first warning signal of a change in direction, with a stronger warning occurring if prices break below their previous bottom.

Before leaving the subject of support and resistance, we should state one final rule: Once a support or resistance level has been attacked, it is weakened. It may resist a second attack, but the third attack will usually break through.

12

MOMENTUM

Momentum is simply the rate of change—the *speed* or *slope* at which a stock or commodity ascends or declines. It is calculated by taking the difference between prices separated by a fixed interval of time. For example, today's 5-day momentum value would be today's price minus the price recorded 5 days ago; yesterday's would be yesterday's price minus that of 5 days before yesterday and so on. Expressed mathematically:

$$M(5)_T = \text{Price of today - price of 5 days ago}$$
$$\text{or } M(5)_T = P_T - P_{T-5}$$

Let's take a hypothetical example:

DAY	PRICE	5-DAY MOMENTUM
1	500	---
2	508	---
3	510	---
4	515	---
5	510	---
6	495	-5
7	508	0
8	526	16
9	528	13
10	540	30

One basic way to use a momentum indicator is to buy when it becomes positive and sell when it turns negative. Logically, you are buying when the market is picking up momentum and selling when that momentum is lost. The problem is that, by definition, you're entering the market *after* it has made its turn. But even if you miss the beginning of the move, you should catch most of it, if indeed the market is turning. Later, this should also allow you to exit the market with a profit before prices actually start moving against you in earnest:

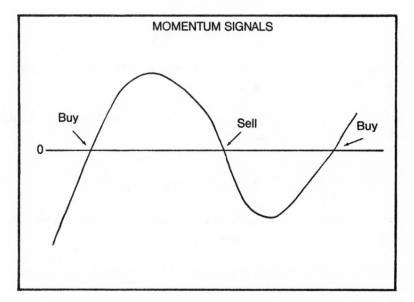

Figure 12-1

CYCLES AND MOMENTUM. One school of thought contends that in order for a momentum indicator to be valid, it must be based on *cycle length*. If it is, it will measure the rate of change of prices within a cycle.

Cycles are found by measuring from one bottom to the next. Cycles are sometimes consistent and easy to spot while at other times they are very difficult to find. Let us assume we have checked on the recent history of a market and have found that it consistently makes a bottom every 20 days or so. The rule states that our calculation of momentum should be set at one-half the days in the cycle, or in this case, 10 days.

This concept can be taken even further by following *three* momentum indicators at the same time–the 10-day momentum *plus* one at 1/4 of the cycle (5 days) and one at the full cycle (20 days). Thus, you will be plotting a 5-day, 10-day and 20-day momentum simultaneously on the same graph. (For more on cycles, see Chapters 23, 24 and 25.)

Up to this point, we can summarize the theory of momentum indicators as follows:

Rising Prices:

1. When the momentum indicator is above zero and moving up, *upward momentum is increasing.*

2. When the momentum indicator is above zero and moving down, *upward momentum is decreasing.*

Declining Prices:

3. When the momentum indicator is below zero and moving down, *downward momentum is increasing.*

4. When the momentum indicator is below zero and moving up, *downward momentum is decreasing.*

OSCILLATORS. A completely different approach to the use of momentum indicators attempts to anticipate the end of a move when momentum is either "too high" or "too low." These conditions, respectively, are known as "overbought" and "oversold." The idea is that, in an overbought condition, nearly all investors who have had any intention of buying this particular stock or commodity have probably *already* committed all or most of the money they intend to commit for the time being; while in an oversold condition, they have *already* done most of the their selling. The general rule is to sell when the momentum indicator shows an overbought reading and buy when an oversold condition is indicated. (Figure 12-2).

Momentum may be zero, positive or negative. If a market is at the same price after 5 days, the 5-day momentum will be zero. If it is higher, the momentum is positive; and if lower, negative. The key question is this:

Is there a maximum positive or negative value for momentum? In commodity markets the answer is *yes*. There is usually a specified, mandatory limit as to how much a price is allowed to move each day. So, in this case, the maximum 5-day momentum would generally be that daily limit multiplied by 5.

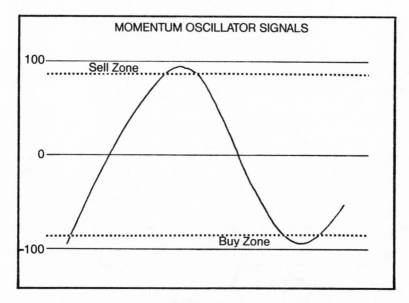

Figure 12-2

A momentum indicator used in this way is referred to as an "oscillator." The momentum indicator we have been discussing, however, is not an oscillator in its present form. It must first be "normalized," which means that all values must be converted to a range between +1 and -1, or +100% and -100%. To accomplish this, we divide the momentum value by the maximum obtainable momentum value. For example, in the T-bill market, the limit for one day is 60 points. Using a 5-day momentum would give us a maximum obtainable momentum of 300. Thus, a momentum value of 150 would translate into an oscillator value of +0.5 or +50%.

Figures 12-3, 12-4 and 12-5 show a 5-day momentum, a 5-day momentum oscillator, and combined 5, 10 and 20-day momentum oscillators.

Bear in mind that any limit we set—whether based upon actual market

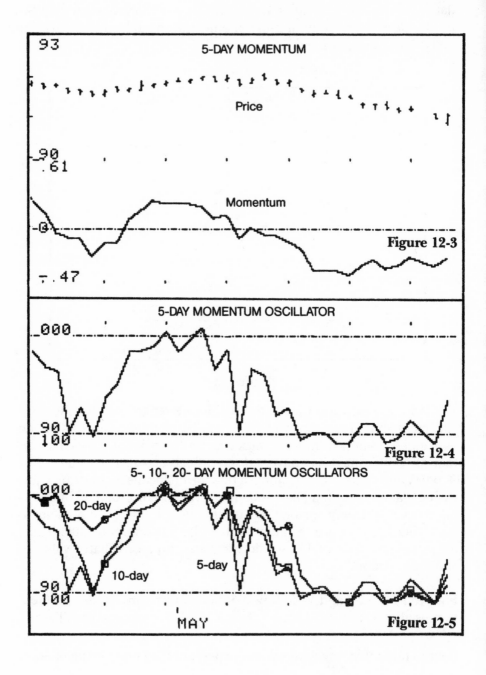

93
5-DAY MOMENTUM

Price

90
.61

Momentum

Figure 12-3

−.47

5-DAY MOMENTUM OSCILLATOR

000

90
100

Figure 12-4

5-, 10-, 20- DAY MOMENTUM OSCILLATORS

000

20-day

5-day

10-day

90
100

MAY

Figure 12-5

limits or not—is an arbitrary guideline to give you a general idea of the overbought or oversold condition. A more valid way to set limits is to run the momentum indicator for approximately one year of history and use the indicator's highs and lows of that period as your maximum and minimum.

It is very easy, with a computer, to develop a trading system using over-bought/oversold oscillators. These would be the logical steps to follow:

1. Select how many days to use for momentum.

2. Decide on one or more oscillators.

3. Define the maximum ranges—what will constitute an overbought or oversold condition.

4. Construct trading rules.

Some examples of different trading rules might be:

1. Sell when the 5-day oscillator goes above 0.9 or 90%.

2. Sell when the 5-day oscillator stays above 90% for 2 days.

3. Sell when both the 5-day and 10-day oscillators are above 90%.

In short, momentum indicators can be used to trade with the trend when they cross the zero line or against the trend when they hit a peak. Be aware that when you are either selling into an overbought condition or buying into a oversold condition, you are categorically bucking the short-term trend. You are betting on what your oscillators claim is a high pro-bability of a technical reaction occurring. Accordingly, this type of method is best suited to very short-term trading. In developing a trading system based on momentum, we would prefer to trade *with* the trend. Overbought/oversold oscillators do, however, provide indispensable technical information to the analyst—we wouldn't be without them.

13

MOVING AVERAGES

Moving averages are used to determine when a trend has changed direction and are the basis of many trend-following systems. In a simple three-day moving average, for example, we add the three most recent days and divide by three. Thus, if today is Wednesday, the moving average for today would be the average price of Monday, Tuesday and Wednesday. Then, on Thursday, we would drop off Monday's price and take the average of Tuesday, Wednesday and Thursday; and so on. The formula for a simple 3-day moving average (M3) would be:

$$M3 = \frac{P_T + P_{T-1} + P_{T-2}}{3}$$

Where P_T equals today's close; P_{T-1} equals yesterday's close; and P_{T-2} equals the close of the day before yesterday. Table 13-1 shows a hypothetical example:

TABLE 13-1. BUILDING A 3-DAY MOVING AVERAGE

Day	Price	3-day moving average
1	5	--
2	6	--
3	7	6
4	9	7.33
5	11	9

The simple moving average gives equal weight to each price in the sample.

A WEIGHTED MOVING AVERAGE on the other hand, can be used to give more significance to the most recent price, the earliest price or the middle price in the group. Another popular type of weighting factor is known as *exponential smoothing* which can be calculated for you automatically with a computer.

Prepackaged software is readily available to compute both simple and exponentially-smoothed moving averages. In addition, such software usually lets you set the number of days (or weeks or months as the case may be) in the moving average. As the number of days in the moving average increases, the moving average becomes smoother, less responsive to short-term fluctuations and, thus, slower to respond to changes in trend. The advantage is that you will experience fewer false starts; and the primary disadvantage is that much of the price move will have already taken place by the time the slow moving average has signaled a change. Your diligent research in this area will tell you which moving average shows optimum results for each stock or commodity you wish to trade. This is the first step toward developing a moving average system.

Moving Average Systems

A moving average system is a set of trading rules that are applied to moving averages. On the same chart you may be interested in:

(a) the relationship between price and moving average, or

(b) the relationship between two or more moving averages themselves.

The most basic way to use a moving average is to simply interpret a change of direction in a single moving average as a signal to buy or sell. (Figure 13-1).

However, this is perhaps *too* simple. A more common approach would be to study the relationship between actual price and a single moving average. In the stock market, when a stock price is above its 200-day moving average, it is considered a bullish sign. (Shorter-term signals

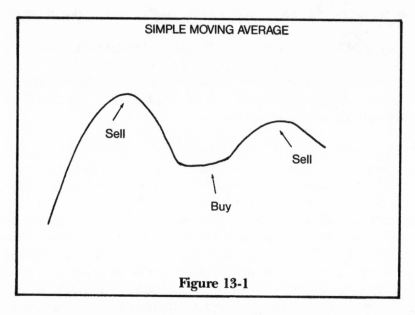

Figure 13-1

would be generated using a 10- or 20-day moving average.) The basic strategy would be as follows: Buy when prices cross *above* the moving average. Sell when prices cross *below* the moving average. Typically, you may wish to use closing prices only:

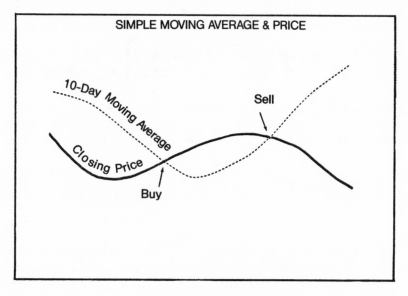

Figure 13-2

THE TWO CROSSOVER MODEL is the next step up in level of complexity, making use of two simple moving averages. A typical example would be a 14-day moving average combined with a 50-day moving average. (This particular combination was found to be very effective in the gold market in a study done by Merrill Lynch.) The rule would be: Buy when the 14-day moving average crosses above the 50-day moving average; sell when it crosses below the 50-day moving average.

A modified version of this system would take into account the actual prices as. well. The rules might then be:

(1) Buy when the actual price crosses above *both* moving averages and exit the market when the price crosses below *either* moving average.

(2) Sell short when the actual price crosses below *both* moving averages and exit the market when the price crosses *above either moving average*.

Finally, three or more moving averages may be combined to make a system. Such qualifications usually result in fewer trades and trades of a shorter duration. Moreover, it is probably too complex. Remember, making a system more complex does not necessarily make it a better one.

THE 200-DAY MOVING AVERAGE OF THE DOW illustrated in figure 13-3, is an excellent long-term indicator, and as such may be better utilized by the investor rather than the trader. Its signals, once generated, are seldom wrong over the longer term. If, after both the Dow and the 200-Day Moving Average have been declining for some time, the Dow should move up and cross the Moving Average, it indicates that a new bull market has begun. Later, confirmation of this initial signal occurs when the 200-Day Moving Average itself turns up.

During the first stage of the bull market, both the Dow and the Moving Average move up in concert. Eventually, the Dow suffers its first serious setback which may or may not send prices below the Moving Average. But this does not necessarily signal an end to the bull market. If the market correction is severe, the Moving Average may turn down as well. Again, this does not necessarily mean the bull market has ended. Instead, the Moving Average will usually turn back and go on to new highs.

It is only *after* this *second* leg up in the 200-Day Moving Average that

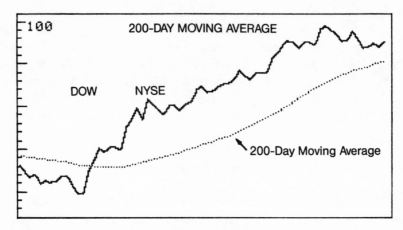

Figure 13-3

you should begin to look for market deterioration and sell signals—an initial crossing *below* the Moving Average by the Dow and then, a decline in the Moving Average itself.

All these moving averages ignore volume. Attempts to evaluate both *price* and volume simultaneously are discussed in the next chapter.

14

ON-BALANCE VOLUME

Earlier, just as studying volume on a day-to-day basis helped us to determine the power of a particular price move, so does On-Balance Volume (OBV) help us to detect patterns of accumulation and distribution.

JOSEPH GRANVILLE calculates it this way: If today's closing price is higher than yesterday's, we add today's volume to a cumulative total. If the closing price is lower, today's volume is subtracted from the total. On days when prices remain unchanged, the cumulative volume also remains unchanged. Here is an example to illustrate the technique:

TABLE 14-1. CALCULATING ON-BALANCE VOLUME

DAY	PRICE	VOLUME	ON-BALANCE VOLUME
1	10	7,000	7,000
2	12	5,000	12,000
3	15	8,000	20,000
4	15	4,000	20,000
5	14	5,000	15,000
6	12	3,000	12,000

On-Balance Volume can be equally effective with individual stocks, the stock averages, or individual commodities. Accumulation is indicated by rising OBV; distribution by falling OBV. Since the starting point is arbitrary, the absolute level of the on-balance volume is of no significance. We are only interested in the contour of its curve when it is compared with the contour of the price curve—either graphically or in tabulated form.

For example, let's say prices are moving sideways. Is this an accumulation which will lead to a continuation of the trend? Or is it a distribution which implies that prices will turn around and move in the opposite direction? The OBV can often tell us the true state of affairs. As a rule, the OBV parallels the price. It is only when there is a *divergence* between the OBV and the price that we can tell if accumulation or distribution is occurring. For example, if prices have been moving sideways in a trading range while OBV has been increasing, we would conclude that accumulation was occurring. The rising OBV resulted from more stock being purchased on up days than was sold on down days:

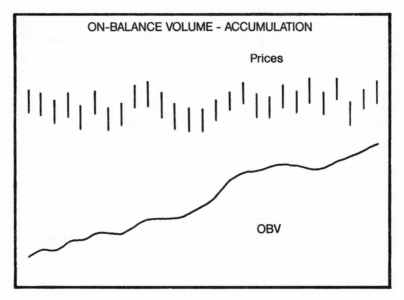

Figure 14-1

Distribution is indicated if prices are moving sideways and the OBV is falling. We could conclude a major top is forming and prices should drop quickly. (Figure 14-2).

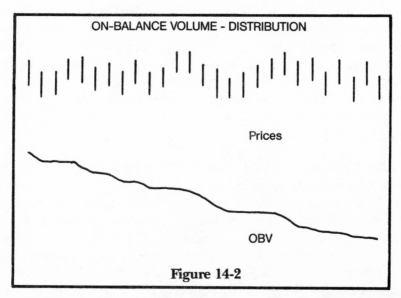

Figure 14-2

What if prices, instead of moving sideways, are in an uptrend while the OBV is moving sideways? Again, we would have a *divergence* between price and OBV. This divergence would indicate that the price rise is not being accompanied by strong volume and that this market is weak and could easily reverse:

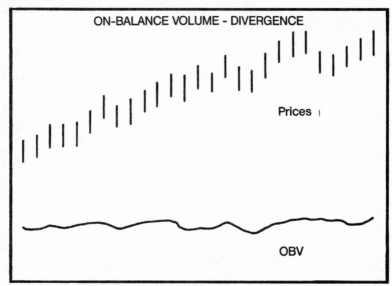

Figure 14-3

Some analysts feel that this method for calculating the basic OBV may be too simplistic. Since each day's price change is determined by transactions on *both* the buying and selling side, they feel it is an exaggeration to assign *all* the volume to the plus or minus side simply because the close one day is higher or lower than the close of the preceding day. Others argue that a more reasonable approach would be to ignore the previous day's close and determine if prices rise or fall from today's open to today's close.

MARK CHAIKEN'S VOLUME ACCUMULATOR is an alternative to the Granville On-Balance Volume System which is supposed to solve this problem. It provides a more sensitive intraday measurement of volume in relation to price action. He does this by placing added emphasis upon the day's close in relation to its average or *mean* price for that day. For example, if the close is above the mean, a percentage of the volume is assigned a positive value. Conversely, if it falls below the mean, a portion is considered negative. If the close is the same as the high, all volume is treated as positive. Likewise, if the close is the same as the low, all volume is treated as negative.

An accumulative line is drawn and, like in Granville's OBV, the trader is advised to look for divergences between this line and the price trend. For example, if the cumulative line fails to confirm an upward trend, a decline in price may be indicated.

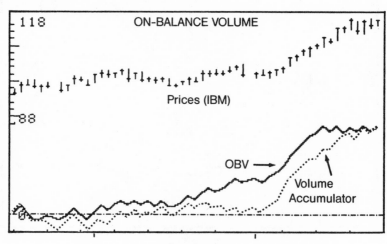

Figure 14-4

Although the Volume Accumulator and Granville's OBV will often agree, this is not always the case. Comparing figure 14-4, you will notice the difference in these two indicators when applied to the same data.

Still, with all its faults, OBV is a very useful tool for spotting accumulation and distribution. For a much more comprehensive study of OBV, traders can refer to Granville's *New Strategy Of Daily Stock Market Trading For Maximum Profit.*

With the array of tools you have mastered regarding price and volume analysis, you have now taken the first important steps towards your goal of consistently winning in the markets. Most of the techniques you have learned can be applied equally well to any market—individual stocks, the Dow Jones averages, gold, silver, soybeans, the German mark, T-bonds—you name it. But when you attempt to analyze the stock market you will need additional tools designed specifically for that purpose.

III

STOCK MARKET

CHAPTER

15

"THE AVERAGES" & DOW THEORY

How is the stock market doing? Sounds like a simple question. But in fact it is an extremely provocative one—one which you will find more difficult to answer with a brief reply the more you learn about the market. Usually the person who poses the question wants to hear "good," "bad," or "indifferent." But for you and I who study the stock market, it's not that simple. A one-word answer tells us nothing about chart patterns, volume, divergences, nonconfirmations of the various averages, the various industry sectors, etc. It doesn't even address the fundamental problem: What is the stock market?

The stock market is really the sum total of *each and every* stock that is traded. The problem is we usually don't measure it that way. Instead we use a variety of market "averages" which reflect far more limited samples of stocks considered representative of the total.

THE DOW JONES INDUSTRIAL AVERAGE is the most popular and tracks the price of 30 large industrial companies, but was never intended by its inventor, Charles H. Dow, to be analyzed or tracked to the exclusion of the other Dow Jones averages—20 transportations, 15 utilities and 65 composite stocks. Nevertheless, it is the Industrials which are the most widely followed of the four and the one usually referred to in summaries of daily stock-market activity.

The broader market averages—the Standard and Poors 500 Stock Index (S&P 500), the New York Stock Exchange Index (NYSE), and sometimes the Value Line Index—are often preferred by market professionals and technical analysts because they are more representative of the overall market than the 30 Dow Jones Industrials.

THE S&P INDEX represents 500 heavily capitalized, bluechip companies.

THE NEW YORK STOCK EXCHANGE INDEX, created in 1966 as a result of criticism that the Dow is not a true reflector of the market, comprises *all* stocks listed on the New York Stock Exchange and is thus the broadest measure of that market.

THE VALUE LINE, is comprised of 1700 stocks listed on various exchanges and is unique in that it is the only "unweighted" average of those discussed here. This means that each stock, regardless of its price, is weighted equally in determining the index value. Thus, by watching this index in relationship to the S&P, for example, you can judge how the secondary, less capitalized companies are doing in relation to the "bluechips."

Dow Theory is not a fancy little formula for which you can buy software. Instead, it is a comprehensive "theory" of stock market behavior. It is, in effect, one of the first major "technical" studies ever attempted on the stock market, and though occasionally criticized, still must be considered to be a valuable tool due to its long record of success in stock-market prognostication.

In 1897, two market averages were compiled. The "Rails," which included 20 railroad companies, have since been broadened to include the airlines and renamed the "Transports." The Industrial Average, representing most other types of business and made up originally of only 12 issues, was increased later to 20 in 1916 and 30 in 1928. In 1929, all stocks of public utility companies were dropped from the Industrial Average and a new Utility Average of 20 issues was set up, and reduced to 15 in 1936. Finally, the three have been averaged together to make the Dow Jones 65 - Stock Composite Index. Traditional Dow Theory pays no attention to the utility or composite averages; its interpretations are based exclusively on the Rails (transports) and Industrials.

There is much to suggest that Charles H. Dow did not think of his theory as a device for forecasting the stock market, but rather as a barometer of general business trends. The basic principles of the theory were outlined by him in editorials he wrote for the *Wall Street Journal*. Upon his death in 1902, his successor as editor of the newspaper, William P. Hamilton, took up Dow's principles and, in the course of 27 years of writing on the market, formulated them into the Dow Theory as we know it today. As you read the basic tenets of the Dow Theory below, you will soon see the origin of basic terminology and theory used in modern-day technical analysis.

1. **THE AVERAGES DISCOUNT EVERYTHING THAT CAN BE KNOWN.** Because the averages reflect the combined market activities of thousands of investors, including those possessing the best foresight and information, the averages in their day-to-day fluctuations discount everything known, everything foreseeable, and every condition which can affect the supply or demand for stocks. Unpredictable happenings such as earthquakes may not be reflected in the averages, but they are soon appraised after they occur. Because of this discounting function, the behavior of the averages affords the first clue as to the future of stock prices.

2. **THE THREE TRENDS.** The three trends that are continually unfolding are the Primary (Major Trend), Secondary (Intermediate Trend), and Day-to-Day (Minor Trend). These trends are sometimes likened to the ocean's tide, waves and ripples.

3. **THE PRIMARY TRENDS.** These broad movements usually last for more than a year and may run for several years, resulting in general appreciation or depreciation in value of more than 20%. So long as each successive rally reaches a higher level than the one before it and each secondary reaction stops at a higher level than the previous reaction,the Primary Trend is up and we are in a *bull market*. Conversely, when each intermediate decline carries prices to successively lower levels and each intervening rally fails to exceed the top of the previous rally, the Primary Trend is down and we are in a *bear market*.

4. **THE SECONDARY TRENDS** are reactions occurring in a bull market and *rallies* occurring in a bear market. Normally, they last from a few weeks to a few months and retrace from one-third to two-thirds of the gain or loss registered by the preceding swing in the Primary Trend.

5. **THE MINOR TRENDS.** The Secondary Trend is composed of Minor Trends or day-to-day fluctuations which are considered unimportant to the Dow theorist. They usually last less than six days but may last up to three weeks.

6. THE BULL MARKET. The Primary Trend usually consists of three phases. The first phase is known as "accumulation" and occurs when business conditions are still poor and the public is generally discouraged with the stock market. The second phase is usually a fairly steady advance on increasing activity as business conditions and corporate earnings begin to improve. The third phase is characterized by highly publicized "good news." Price gains are often spectacular and the public becomes heavily involved.

7. THE BEAR MARKET. Primary down trends are also usually characterized by three phases. The first phase, known as distribution, is when farsighted investors sell their shares to the less informed public. The second phase is the panic phase. In this phase buying decreases, selling becomes more urgent, and the downward trend of prices accelerates on mounting volume. After the panic phase, there may be a fairly long secondary recovery or a sidewise movement. Finally, the business news begins to deteriorate and prices resume their decline though less rapidly than before. The bear market ends when everything possible in the way of bad news has been discounted.

8. PRINCIPLE OF CONFIRMATION. No valid signal of a change in trend can be generated by either the industrials or rails (transports) independent of the other. In other words, if one average makes a new high over its previous peak but the other average falls short of exceeding its previous peak, a nonconfirmation has occurred. The move must be considered suspect until both averages confirm by exceeding their previous peaks.

9. VOLUME. In bull markets volume tends to increase on rallies and decrease on declines. But, in Dow Theory, *conclusive* signals as to the market's trend can only be produced by price movement. Volume only affords collateral evidence which may aid interpretation of otherwise doubtful situations.

10. LINES. A Line refers to a sidewise movement in one or both of the averages, which lasts from a few weeks to a few months, in the course of which price fluctuates within a range of approximately 5%. A Line can substitute for a Secondary Trend. A breakout from the Line area is usually significant. It cannot be known in advance which way the breakout will occur, but more often than not, it is in the direction of the trend.

11. **CLOSING PRICES.** Dow Theory pays no attention to any extreme highs or lows which may be registered intraday, but takes into account only the closing figures.

12. **A TREND IN EFFECT CONTINUES UNTIL REVERSED.** This final tenet simply means that once a new primary trend is definitely signaled by the action of the two averages, the odds that it will continue, despite any near-term reactions, are at their greatest. But as the Primary Trend carries on, the odds in favor of its further extension grow smaller.

16

BREADTH OF MARKET INDICATORS

THE ADVANCE-DECLINE LINE is the most common measure of market breadth and is considered to be one of the most important technical indicators of the condition of the stock market. It is derived by taking the difference between the number of advancing issues and the number of declining issues each day. This daily figure is then added or subtracted each day to a cumulative number in order to determine the advance-decline line.

The purpose is to tell you if the market *as a whole* is gaining strength or losing strength—a measure which will often signal a major change in the direction of the market before any of the averages. As an example, when the Dow is advancing, yet the advance-decline line is falling, it means that even though the Dow is up, a majority of the *other* stocks is declining—a warning that the "technical condition" of the market is deteriorating and that the bull market is in "poor health."

Conversely, if the Dow is falling, yet the advance-decline line is rising, it implies that even though the Dow stocks are declining, a majority of other stocks are beginning to advance—a good signal that the market is technically strong and may turn upward shortly.

The theory behind the advance-decline line can best be understood by the "bathtub" analogy. Picture the market as a bathtub and the water level as represented by the advance-decline line. Advancing stocks raise the water level and declining stocks lower the water level. Market strength or weakness is determined by that water level.

The "smart money" is always the first to get out when the water level of the market stops rising and starts to come down, even though the

Dow may still be in an uptrend. This smart money is the first "water" to flow out the drain. Likewise, the "dumb money" is the last water to leave the tub -- when the flow is speeded up, panic selling takes place and the lowest prices are reached in one last precipitous drop.

At that time, the bear market has ended and a new bull market is about to begin. Just as the smart money was the first to leave the bathtub when it was full, it is also the smart money which will be the first to flow back when it is empty.

The smart money then becomes the bottom layer of water, the foundation upon which the new bull market will be built, and on which all the other layers of water will rest. Thus, smart money is the first in and first out; while dumb money, sitting up on the surface, is last in, last out.

Simple enough so far. But a little more study reveals that we must also consider *which phase* of the bull or bear market we are in and whether we are attempting to predict a market top or market bottom.

The first phase of a bull market is characterized by a rising advance-decline line as the smart money enters the market.

In the second phase, the advance-decline line also trends higher but usually tops out late in the second phase or early in the third phase as the smart money begins to get out.

In the third phase, it should clearly complete its rise, signalling the end of the bull market. The advance-decline line then trends lower throughout the first two phases of the new bear market and most, if not all, of the third phase.

We find that the advance-decline line indicator is much better at picking market tops than market bottoms. Market tops are always forewarned by a declining advance-decline line. During bear market bottoms, however, the advance-decline line often turns up at the same time as the Dow and sometimes even later with a certain lag. Notice in figure 16-1 how the advance-decline line gave no warning that the market was about to bottom in August 1982.

Here's a recap of the possible advance/decline situations. (Remember to take into consideration what phase the market appears to be in. Also, never rely solely on one indicator alone.)

TABLE 16-1. ADVANCE/DECLINE INDICATOR

DOW	ADVANCE/DECLINE LINE	PROGNOSIS
Rising prices	Falling	Lower
Approaching or at previous top	Considerably below corresponding top	Lower prices
Approaching or at previous top	Considerably above corresponding top	Still higher prices
Falling	Rising*	Higher prices
Approaching or at previous bottom	Considerably above previous bottom	Higher prices
Approaching or at previous bottom	Considerably below previous bottom	Still lower prices

---

*Time lag possible here. Should be used more as a confirming than a forecasting tool.

The advance-decline line in its "raw" form is shown in Figure 16-1. It is simply a cumulative sum of advances minus declines.

Some analysts prefer the smoothing effects of a moving average, with a 10-day moving average commonly used (see Figure 16-2).

THE UNCHANGED ISSUES INDEX is also a valuable tool. Sometimes it is useful to watch not only the numbers of stocks that advance and decline but also the number that remain unchanged. In theory, when a higher than normal percentage of stocks remain unchanged in price, the market is likely making a top. The index is calculated each day by dividing the number of issues which are unchanged in price by the total number of stocks traded. The percentage derived from the calculation will usually fluctuate in a range between 5% and 25%. Readings near the low end of the range are considered bullish, while readings near the high end are bearish.

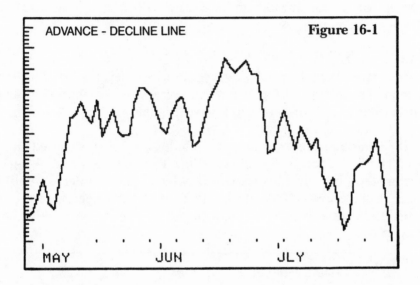

ADVANCE - DECLINE LINE   Figure 16-1

MAY   JUN   JLY

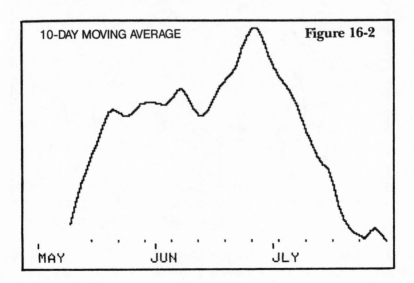

10-DAY MOVING AVERAGE   Figure 16-2

MAY   JUN   JLY

Advanced Indicators

Over the years, many analysts have developed sophisticated breadth indices by *combining* volume with advance-decline data. The remainder of this chapter explores eight unique market breadth indices, each developed by a different analyst. The material is quite technical and is included here as a reference for those who might want to explore the concept of market breadth more deeply. Others may wish to skip to the next chapter.

THE HAURLAN INDEX developed by Dave Holt, publisher of *Trade Levels,* takes the advance/decline concept one step further. This index is made up of three different moving averages which flash short-term, intermediate, and long-term buy or sell signals.

In the Haurlan Index, the short-term index is a 3-day weighted moving average of advances over declines. When the index moves above + 100, a short-term buy signal is generated, which remains in effect until the index drops below -150 at which time a sell signal is generated. The sell signal then remains in effect until the index moves above + 100 again and so on:

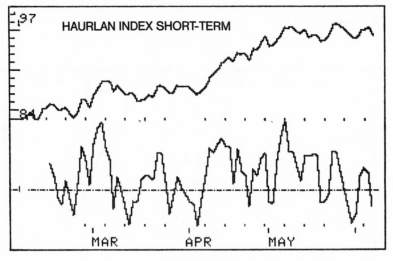

Figure 16-3

The Haurlan Intermediate Term Index is a 20-day weighted moving average, interpreted the same way you would interpret any price chart.

Buy and sell signals are determined by the crossing of trend lines or support/resistance levels:

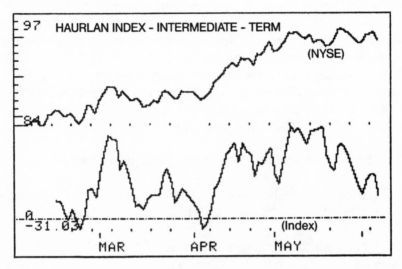

Figure 16-4

The Long-term Index—a 200-day weighted moving average of net advances over declines—is used to measure the primary trend of the market and not to determine precisely timed buy and sell points:

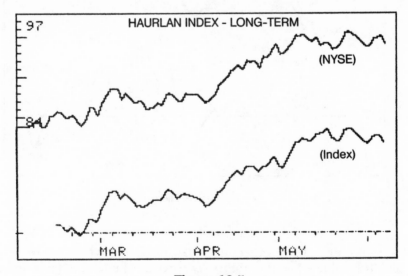

Figure 16-5

THE McCLELLAN OSCILLATOR and SUMMATION INDEX developed in the late '60s by Sherman and Marian McClellan, represent another approach to the advance/decline concept. They are a short-to intermediate-term indicator of market behavior, pointing out overbought and oversold conditions. They use the same advance-decline line, but take the difference between the equivalent of a weighted 20-day moving average and a weighted 40-day moving average. This then behaves like an oscillator, fluctuating between a maximum and minimum range, forming chart patterns which are useful in forecasting market turns and the duration of market moves.

The McClellan Oscillator has two important characteristics:

1. The oscillator reaches an extreme value, measuring overbought and oversold conditions, *before* important turning points.

2. The oscillator then passes through zero at or very soon *after* the turning points:

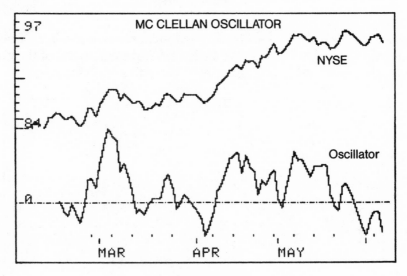

Figure 16-6

The Summation Index—a cumulative total of each day's McClellan Oscillator value—has the ability to forecast the longer term trend of the market (Figure 16-7).

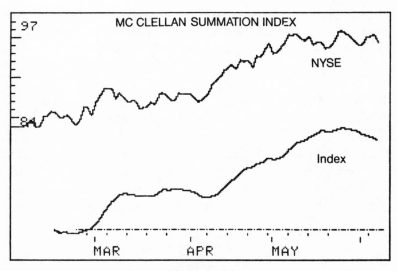

Figure 16-7

Figure 16-8 shows the position of the Summation Index at the August 1982 market bottom. Notice how it failed to go lower than in June.

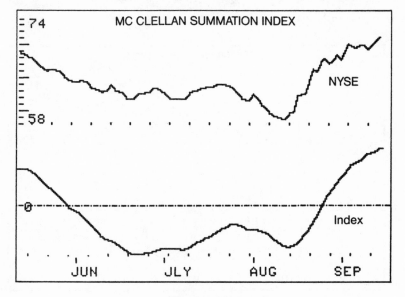

Figure 16-8

A 50-page booklet, *Patterns for Profit*, detailing how to use and interpret both the McClellan Oscillator and Summation Index is available from Trade Levels, Inc., 21241 Ventura Boulevard, Suite 269, Woodland Hills, CA 91364.

THE ARMS INDEX is among those that take the breadth of market studies one step further by adding *volume* to the equation. It measures the relative strength of volume entering advancing stocks against the strength of volume entering declining stocks, and is calculated as follows: Divide the number of advancing stocks by the number of declining stocks. Then divide the upside volume by the downside volume. Finally, divide the first answer by the second result. Expressed in a formula:

$$X = (A/D) / (UV/DV)$$

where X = Arms Index
A = advancing stocks
D = declining stocks
UV = upside volume
DV = downside volume

This gives you the short-term index. Readings below 1.0 are bullish; readings above 1.0 are bearish. Extreme readings of 1.50 or higher are very bearish; and of .50 or lower very bullish. "Climax readings" would be at 2.00 and .30.

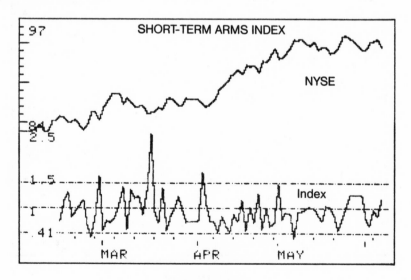

Figure 16-9

A short-to-medium term trading signal can be obtained by plotting a 5-day moving average of the short-term index. Here, a sell signal is generated when the index rises above 1.00; a buy signal produced when it falls below 1.00.

An intermediate to long-term trading signal can be generated by using a 10 day moving average of the index and, as such, it may be viewed as an overbought/oversold indicator. A longer term signal can be pro-

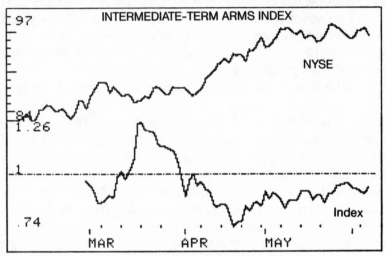

Figure 16-10

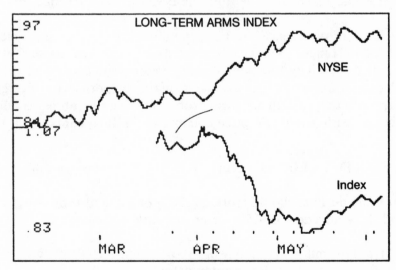

Figure 16-11

duced by using a 10-day/25-day moving average crossover of the index. On the resulting graphs (see figures 16-9, 16-10 and 16-11) you can also use trendline and support/resistance theory. (More information on this system can be found in Gerald Appel's *Winning Stock Selection Systems*, published by Signalert Corporation, Great Neck, New York.)

THE HUGHES BREADTH INDICATOR is the result of some of the most exhaustive work on market breadth conducted by James F. Hughes. He used an advance-decline ratio which is derived by subtracting the number of declines from the number of advances and then dividing that number by the total issues traded. The following conclusions were abstracted from his *Weekly Market Letter*, written from 1960 to 1964 while at the New York firm of Auchincloss, Parker & Redpath.

Hughes believed that sustained major advances in the market are completely dependent upon a harmonious relationship between breadth and price. Indeed, he found good reason to be concerned whenever the breadth index began to decline while the Dow Jones Averages continued to advance. His research showed that all major declines since 1919 were preceded by three to ten weeks of a declining trend in the breadth index, during which period the DJIA could stage at least two rallies to new highs without confirmation by the indicator. Following such a divergence, the DJIA would generally decline to levels *below* the price level it had reached at the time the breadth index reached *its* high.

Such major divergences do not generally occur in markets which are in trading ranges. Rather, they are associated with periods of high speculative activity following sustained advances. Therefore, although relatively rare, when they do occur, major breadth/price divergences carry with them a high technical probability that the subsequent decline will end with a multiple price collapse or "selling climax."

A SELLING CLIMAX occurs under the following circumstances:

(a) Daily declines should represent 70% or more of total issues traded and daily advances of 15% or less of total issues traded.

(b) Until the market has a day or two of visible technical recovery, consecutive climax days are counted as only *one* selling climax.

(c) Following one selling climax, if a rally fails to gain 50% of the ground lost during the decline, the decline should resume. If a second climax appears, the rally objective is raised to two-thirds of the decline. And, following a triple selling climax, technical probabilities highly favor a twenty percent rally from the lows. Until you have an indication of at least three selling climaxes, there is no justification for buying. But, as a general rule, whenever five temporary selling climaxes are crowded into thirty-five days or less, the investor can purchase stocks for a move up of intermediate proportions.

As we saw earlier in the chapter, the failure of our breadth indicators to confirm a new high in the Dow implied lower prices. But it does not necessarily mean that a *major* decline is imminent. Such nonconfirmation has frequently preceded relatively *minor* intermediate trading swings. However, it can be very helpful because as long as the breadth is continuing to make new highs, even if the Dow is not, a bear market is highly unlikely; and, any reaction which develops without a divergence must be regarded as only an intermediate interruption of an uptrend, (This is supported by documentation which goes back as far as 1934).

A BUYING CLIMAX, although not defined by Hughes, can be characterized with criteria which are similar to those of the selling climax: Advancing issues representing 70% or more of total issues and declining issues 15% or less. Since a buying climax takes place generally near intermediate bottoms—not the ultimate tops—and is often followed by new highs, its significance is not as great as a selling climax.

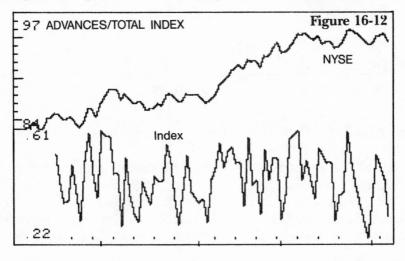

Figure 16-12

We have programmed our computer to look for selling climaxes and find it to be quite accurate in spotting short-term oversold conditions that are likely to result in a bounceback the next day (Figure 16-12).

RICHARD RUSSELL, publisher of *Dow Theory Letters*, is well known for his work on breadth. Like Hughes, he also uses the advance/decline ratio which he computes by subtracting the number of declining issues and dividing the result by the total issues traded (A - D)/T. Like Hughes, Russell rates this indicator highly, writing that: "In general, I have found the AD ratio to be the dominant indicator or the more reliable indicator of the primary trend of the market. Thus highs on breadth unconfirmed by highs on the Industrial Average generally occur only within a primary bull market. Conversely, new lows on the Industrial Average generally occur within the framework of primary bear markets":

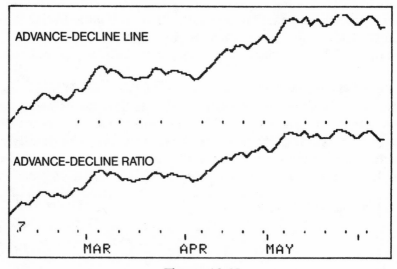

Figure 16-13

The **A/D LINE** is not significantly different from the A/D RATIO.

PAUL DYSART, editor of *Trendway Economic Services*, uses the basic advance-decline line which he calls his Composite Basic Issues Traded Index. He takes this idea one step further in his creation of a Positive Volume Issues Traded Index (PVITI) and a Negative Volume Issues Traded Index (NVITI). The former is the summation of advances minus declines *only on days when total volume of trading increases over that of the previous day.* The latter is defined similarly on days when volume of trading *decreased* from the previous day, and it is this one which Dysart feels is the most valuable since it measures the way the market regains its equilibrium after the effect of increased volume days:

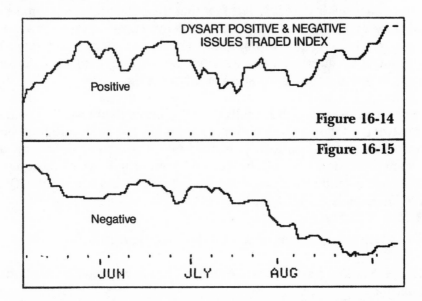

DYSART POSITIVE & NEGATIVE ISSUES TRADED INDEX

Positive

Figure 16-14

Figure 16-15

Negative

JUN   JLY   AUG

HAMILTON BOLTON, the late editor of the *Bolton-Tremblay Bank Credit Analyst,* was one of the few analysts who calculated an advance-decline index using the *unchanged* issues as a basic component. He used the square root of the difference between the ratio of advances to unchanged and the ratio of declining to unchanged (BOLTON INDEX = square root of A/U - D/U). His reasons for the square root was that it eliminated a strong downward bias.

In dynamic up and down phases of the market, Bolton's index is impacted by (1) heavy excesses of advances over declines or vice versa, and (2) a shrinking, unchanged component in the denominator. In top areas, however, and in slow bottom areas, unchanged issues tend to expand, reducing the index. Such action helps indicate a turn in trend and supports the contention of underlying strength or weakness.

WALTER HEIBY, in his exhaustive book on market breadth, *Stock Market Profits Through Dynamic Synthesis,* concludes that the usual breadth-of-market studies are not complete and do not always hold true. He points to the 1963-64 period when the number of advancing issues each day was a continual disappointment, leading many analysts to expect a major decline which never materialized; and he suggests that the breadth indicators in those years reflected high institutional demand for Dow Jones quality stocks. The fact that the public refused to make the advance a broader one should not have swayed the investor from a bullish posture. Heiby's point has become particularly relevant in today's environment of uncertainty and with institutions accounting for an increasingly larger percentage of stock market trading.

Heiby's answer, which he calls the "Dynamic Synthesis," essentially involves the following steps: First, he takes the last 50-day trading period and splits the chart into four horizontal quartiles—top, bottom, and two in the middle. Second, he looks for four criteria which must be met to obtain a valid buy signal which he calls the "Advance-Decline Quartile Divergence Syndrome."

To obtain a buy signal, four criteria must be met:

1. The Standard and Poor Composite Index must be in the bottom quartile.

2. The Advancing Issues Index must be in the top quartile.

3. The Advancing Issues Index must be greater than the Declining Issues Index.

4. The unchanged Issues must not be in the top quartile.

Similarly, to obtain a sell signal, five criteria must be met:

1. The Standard and Poor Composite Index must be in the top quartile.

2. The Advancing Issues Index must be in the bottom quartile.

3. The Declining Issues Index must be in the top quartile.

4. The Advancing Issues Index must be less than the Declining Issues Index.

5. The Unchanged Issues Index must not be in the lowest quartile.

Finally, after one or another of these sets of criteria have been met, he looks at other indicators such as short sales, odd-lot sales, and odd-lot purchase volume.

17

LEADERSHIP AND QUALITY

During a stock-market rise, determining the quality of stocks leading the advance often can lend an important clue as to what phase it is in. In general, bull markets begin with the high quality blue chips. Then, after a correction, somewhat lower priced stocks are thought to be bargains and rapidly gain investor attention. By the third and final phase of the market advance, the cheaper, more speculative issues—often found on the over-the-counter market or the American Exchange—now make the most rapid gains. This is usually an indication that the bull market is nearing its end.

THE MOST ACTIVE ISSUES is one of the best ways to monitor market leadership. The 15 Most Active Issues (published daily) and the 20 Most Active Issues (published weekly) list which stocks are being most actively bought and sold according to the number of shares traded. Therefore, the lists generally reflect the concentration of big money flows.

How do we determine a quality stock? Price is the best measure; and for the purpose of analysis, we can arbitrarily set the $40 mark as the key threshold: If the majority of the Most Actives has a price of greater than $40 per share, we would consider the advance to be led by *quality* stocks. On the other hand, if the majority of the Most Actives are below $40 per share, with some in the $10-25 price range, we would consider the advance to be primarily speculative, leading us to expect a possible stock-market decline.

When attempting to catch short-term swings, you plot the percentage of the 15 Most Actives that showed a gain for that day. As an example, if 10 issues rise, 2 decline and 3 issues remain unchanged, you would plot 10/15 or 67%. Then you take a 10-day moving average of those percentages.

When the indicator reaches the 60-70% region and starts to turn down, the market will usually be overbought and due for at least a short-term correction. However, if the indicator exceeds 70%, an entirely different signal is flashed and a powerful advance can be expected.

Likewise, when the indicator descends to 30-35% and begins to turn up, the market will be oversold and due for at least a short-term rally. During bear markets, readings of 30% are more usual (Figure 17-1).

Generally we find that divergences between the trend of the indicator and the trend of the market can also be used to help call turning points. If the indicator is rising while prices are falling, expect the market to turn up. Conversely, if the indicator is falling while the market is rising, expect the market to turn down.

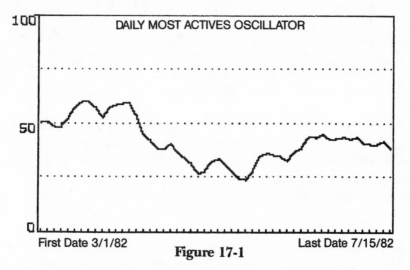

Figure 17-1

Another shorter term indicator using the 15 Most Active Issues is employed by *Indicator Digest* (451 Grand Ave., Palisades Park, NJ 07650). To compute the indicator, simply subtract declining issues from advancing issues. For example, if 10 rose, 4 declined and 1 remained unchanged, the net for the day is 6. If 5 rose, 8 declined and 2 remained unchanged, the net would be -3.

Maintain a 30-day cumulative total of the latest 30 days'' reading. As illustrated in figure 17-2, a buy signal is generated when the 30-day total rises to +9; a sell signal is generated when the 30-day total falls to below -9; and readings between +9 and -9 are neutral, meaning that the previous signal remains in effect.

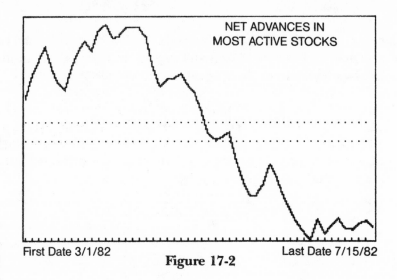

First Date 3/1/82   Last Date 7/15/82

Figure 17-2

NEW HIGHS AND NEW LOWS. This indicator, like the advance-decline line, is also a breadth-of-the-market indicator and can be used in much the same way. "New highs" are defined as the number of issues that have made new highs during the latest 52-week period; whereas "new lows" designate the number of issues that have made new lows during that period.

For instance, if the number of new highs is expanding, it can be considered a bullish sign. If the number of new highs is contracting, while the number of new lows is expanding, it may be considered bearish. The problem is that this interpretation is a bit oversimplified; you really must also consider other factors or it can lead you astray. You must be aware of what phase the market is in and whether divergence exists between your high/low indicator and the market itself.

Let's assume that the Dow Jones has been entrenched in a bear market for two years and your indicator is showing zero stocks at new highs and 650 stocks at new lows. A month later the Dow Jones has plummeted another 50 points, but now the indicator shows 5 stocks at new highs and only 500 stocks at new lows. This is exactly what we are looking for—a major nonconfirmation. It means that 150 stocks have rallied from their lows – an extremely significant event, signalling the end of the bear market. But the context in which all this has occurred is the key. Since the bear market has been in force for two years and since the entire stock-market cycle is typically 4 - 4 1/2 years, we are overdue for a turnaround. If the bear market had recently begun, we would not attach much significance to a similar pattern. Figure 17-3 shows the pattern of new highs and new lows during the critical summer of 1982 prior to the record-smashing rally which soon ensued.

Now, assume a new bull market has begun. At first, the new lows still outnumber the new highs. But we are concerned only with the trend— the fact that each day there are *more* new highs and *fewer* new lows. After four months, the Dow Jones has risen 150 points and our high/low indicator looks healthy. We now have 550 new highs and zero new lows.

One month later, the Dow Jones is 50 points higher but the high/low indicator shows only 400 new highs and 10 new lows. Should we be concerned? Is this the end of the bull market? Maybe not. If, in fact, we are correct in identifying the last major bottom and we are truly in a new bull market, it could be too early for it to be terminating. Rather than a new bear market, our high/low indicator is probably signalling a correction.

It is normal after the first major advance in a bull market for the number of new highs to decrease somewhat—usually as the Dow Jones is entering its first corrective phase. However, if the Dow continues to advance despite a declining number of new highs, it often indicates that a more severe correction is in the making.

To complete the cycle, assume we are 2 - 2 1/2 years into the bull market. We're on the lookout for a turnaround and we detect a serious divergence between the Dow Jones and the high/low indicator: The Dow Jones is still moving higher while the number of new highs is declining. This time, the nonconfirmation can be taken more seriously. Although the peaking out of the number of new highs usually occurs months in advance of the final high in the Dow, this is a good time to begin an orderly liquidation process.

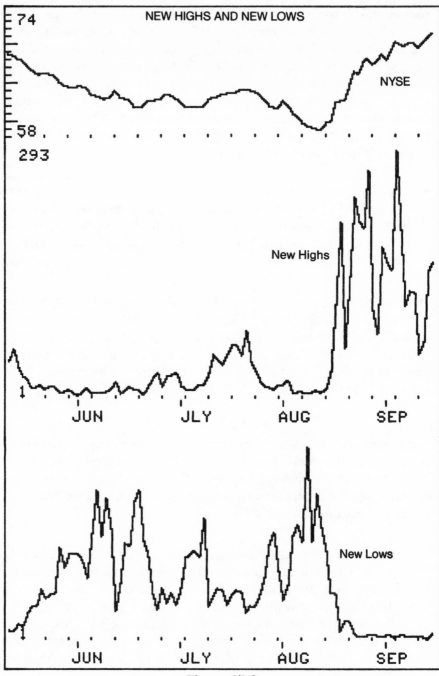

Figure 17-3

Thus, the high/low indicator can be a valuable tool—*if used properly and in conjunction with other indicators.*

We now move to an area which we consider to be among the most important if you are going to properly time the markets, namely **market sentiment.**

18

MARKET SENTIMENT INDICATORS

Market sentiment indicators are those which attempt to gauge the mood of market participants—generally classified as either "sophisticated" or "unsophisticated."

Sophisticated market players are professionals who make their living from stock-market trading. The specialists, for example, concentrate on only one or two issues and trade on the floor of the Exchange for their own account. In order to give each stock better liquidity and to make a more orderly market for the general public, they are required to buy in the absence of other competing bids and to sell in the absence of other competing offers.

Another group, the Exchange members, are those who have purchased a "seat" on the Exchange. This allows them to trade on the floor without paying commissions.

Although there are, of course, many notable exceptions, as a whole, the general public is most often thought to be unsophisticated and, more often than not, wrong in the world of stock-market trading. Therefore, their activity is also watched very closely for a clue as to where the market may be headed.

Professionals consider market sentiment indicators to be among their most valuable tools. The indicators in this chapter will enable you to determine the "mood" of each of the three groups of market participants discussed.

The **SHORT INTEREST RATIO**, published monthly in *Barron's*, is designed to spot when the public becomes overly pessimistic. It is calculated by dividing the total number of short sales outstanding on the NYSE by the average daily trading volume on the exchange that month. If the short interest ratio is above 1.75, it is considered a bullish signal. A reading of slightly above 2.0 (a short interest of twice the average daily volume) was recorded in June of 1982, two months ahead of the dynamic rally that followed in August. Another time the ratio had reached 2.0 was in July 1970, also a very good time to buy stocks.

On the opposite side of the spectrum, the indicator has, on occasion, been used to signal excessive public optimism when the ratio has dropped below 1.0. But such bearish signals have turned out to be very unreliable on several occasions. Therefore *we suggest you use the short interest ratio primarily as a buy signal.*

ODD-LOT PURCHASES OR SHORT SALES refer to all transactions that involve less than 100 shares of stock. Since these purchases and sales are usually transacted by the less sophisticated market players, these figures, published daily in most newspapers, can often play a role in market timing.

It is not too difficult to compute this ratio.   You can do so by dividing odd-lot short sales by total short sales each week. A moving average may then be used to smooth the data.

The basic theory is that a trend toward increased odd-lot selling is bullish; a trend toward decreased odd-lot selling is bearish. You may also look at the other side of the coin. A trend toward increased odd-lot buying is bearish; a trend toward decreased odd-lot buying is bullish.

It has been found that odd-lotters often tend to panic and sell at the wrong times, with odd-lot short selling reaching a peak just as the market bottoms and still a second peak often reached as the market retests its bottom.

SPECIALIST SHORT SALES—by members of the New York Stock Exchange—is a good indicator of the "smart money movements." Since the specialist's purpose is to make an orderly market, he is restricted in trading activity by certain rules. Still, he is considered to be one of the most astute traders in the game, a fact which can be well documented by past performance. Therefore, when heavy specialist short selling is evident, it is usually a good time to be bearish on the market. Conversely, when specialist short selling is light, it often is a good time to be buying stocks. This is not to say that specialists are always right. But, should you notice that specialist short selling is decreasing at the same time as odd-lot short selling is increasing, one indicator is confirming the other, adding credence to the signal.

The Specialist Short Sale Ratio may be computed weekly by dividing the total number of short sales on the NYSE each week into the number of shares sold short by specialists in each week.   These data can also be found in *Barron's*, but there is a two week time lag before the figures are released to the public.

A buy signal can be generated by a single weekly reading below 33%, or a series of four weekly readings averaging below 35%. *A sell signal* is indicated when a single weekly reading exceeds 58% or the average of the latest four weekly readings exceeds 55%. As with the Short Interest Ratio, buy signals tend to be more accurate than sell signals.

MEMBER SHORT SALES also tends to be a good "smart money indicator." Low short selling on the part of the members is considered bullish; heavy short selling is considered bearish. These data are carried weekly and can also be found in *Barron's*.

The Member Short-Sale Ratio is calculated by dividing (a) the number of shares sold short by members of the NYSE by (b) the total number of shares sold short that week (On other occasions, if you want to look at the other side of the coin, you can divide (a) the number of shares sold short by *non*-members of the exchange by (b) total. The result is the "Public Short-Sale Ratio" which, of course, is simply the reciprocal of the Member Short-Sale Ratio.)

It has been found that a reading below 65% in the Member Short-Sale Ratio is usually an excellent buy signal for an intermediate or major move. A study showing this historical relationship was conducted by Norman G. Fosback, in *Stock Market Logic* (The Institute for Economic Research, 3471 N. Federal Highway, Ft. Lauderdale, FL 33306). Here are the results:

TABLE 18-1. MEMBER SHORT SALES AND
THREE-MONTH MARKET PERFORMANCE (1941-75)

Member Short Sales (average of last ten weeks)	S & P 500 Index (3 months later)	Probability of Rising Prices
over 80%	-1.1%	48%
75 - 80%	+0.5%	54%
70 - 75%	+3.3%	68%
65 - 70%	+4.5%	75%
0 - 65%	+5.9%	88%
35-year average	+1.9%	62%

When the 10-week moving average of Member Short Sales was less than 65%, the market's average gain 3 months later was 5.9%; six months later it was 16.5%; and one year later, 24.39%. This indicator also tends to produce better buy signals than sell signals. However, a sale is indicated when the ratio approaches 88%.

MEMBER TRADING, another indicator of member activity, is derived by subtracting the number of shares sold by members of the NYSE from the number purchased. Net buying, designated by a rising line, carries bullish implications. Conversely, a falling line indicates the Members have been selling and should be viewed bearishly. These data are also availably weekly in *Barron's*.

ART MERRILL (Merrill Analysis Inc., Box 228, Chappaqua, NY 10514) has shown that this indicator—using an exponential moving average rather than the raw data—is among the most significant of intermediate and major trend indicators we're aware of . Another approach would be to maintain an exponential moving average of the net weekly cumulative total of member purchases minus sales. You can then chart the difference between the latest week's readings and the exponential moving average you are maintaining. Your indicator will rise as member trading becomes more positive and falls when it turns negative.

ADVISORY SENTIMENT is often best used as an indicator of contrary opinion. It is common knowledge that stock-market investment advisors tend, for the most part, to be trend followers. They tend to turn bullish quite quickly after market prices start rising and to stay bullish during the bull market. Therefore, with some notable exceptions, they cannot be relied upon for calling a market top. Conversely, when the market has been declining, advisors tend to get overly pessimistic, often right at what turns out to be a major bottom. In sum, they seem to do very poorly at the beginning and end of a bear market.

The degree of advisors' optimism and pessimism can best be determined by the "Sentiment Index" which is maintained by *Investors Intelligence* (2 East Avenue, Larchmont, NY 10538). Abe Cohen—the publisher who tallies the percentage of advisory services that are bullish and bearish—has found that bear markets generally touch bottom when 60% or more of advisory services turn outright bearish; but in bull markets, widespread bullish sentiment does not necessarily end the rise.

CUSTOMER'S MARGIN DEBT refers to the amount of money owed to New York Stock Exchange member firms by customers who have borrowed money to finance their stock purchases. This figure, calculated on the last trading day of each month by the NYSE, is not released to the public until two or three weeks later. The figure can be found in *Barron's* or obtained directly by writing to the New York Stock Exchange, 11 Wall Street, New York, NY 10005.

Margin-account traders have traditionally been considered among the more sophisticated stock-market investors. Watching their borrowing patterns reveals when they are buying or selling stocks. When margin debt is rapidly expanding, it indicates that this group is buying heavily; when margin debt is decreasing, it can be reasoned that they are liquidating on balance.

The trend of Customer's Margin Debt has proven to be an excellent long-term market indicator. You can plot a line representing Customer's Margin Debt and also a line representing a 12-month moving average of the same. A buy signal is given when the current figure moves above the 12-month moving average. A sell signal is rendered when the current figure drops below the 12-month moving average. This particular timing method, developed by Norman Fosback, has proven to be an excellent indicator of bull and bear markets during the past 35 years. The important tops of 1956, 1959, 1961, 1966, 1968 and 1973 were all accompanied or preceded by turns in Customer's Margin Debt. Similarly, troughs established in 1957, 1960, 1962, 1966, 1970 and 1974 were accompanied by upturns in Customer's Margin Debt.

FREE CREDIT BALANCES refers to the cash left on account with New York Stock Exchange member brokerage firms. This series is also published monthly and can be obtained either from *Barron's* or directly from the New York Stock Exchange.

Unlike Margin Debt figures, Free Credit Balances usually reflect the activity of smaller, unsophisticated investors. The reasoning behind this is that only unsophisticated investors would allow their cash balances to lie idle at brokerage firms earning no interest.

Rising credit balances indicate that the small investors are selling stock and thus can be interpreted bullishly. Falling credit balances mean small investors are buying and should be interpreted bearishly.

As with Customer's Margin Debt, a useful technique is to plot the current series of Free Credit Balances against a twelve-month moving average. A buy signal is generated when the current series crosses above the twelve-month moving average; a sell signal occurs when the current series crosses below the twelve-month moving average.

DOW JONES UTILITY AVERAGE—Because of their sensitivity to interest rates, the utility stocks are often seen as a bellwether for the entire market. Utility stocks are more sensitive to interest rates than other stocks for two reasons: 1) utilities are heavy borrowers and thus their earnings are easily hurt by rising interest rates; and 2) utilities customarily pay a high dividend yield and are often purchased as a substitute for bonds. When interest rates rise, investors are likely to sell their utility stocks—purchased originally for their yield—and rush to higher yielding short-term instruments such as T-bills. Thus, the Dow Jones Utility Average is often considered to be a leading indicator for the major trend of the stock market.

A useful technique is to plot the Dow Jones Utility Average overlayed with a 15-week moving average. When the current readings are above the 15-week moving average, the utility stocks can be classified as being in an uptrend and the stock market also should continue higher. When current readings drop below the 15-week moving average, a sell signal is in order.

Market sentiment indicators—like the others considered in this book —are almost exclusively concerned with technical factors which are internal to the market. In the next chapter, however, we give a few examples of how your computer can also track fundamental monetary indicators.

19

MONETARY INDICATORS

NET FREE RESERVES are an important measure of liquidity in the banking system. They represent the excess cash that banks hold over and above their legal required reserves and borrowings from the Federal Reserve (figure 19-1). When banks are flush with funds, the banking system is termed to be in a "net free reserves" position. Under such conditions the banks have the ability to finance business growth and economic expansion.

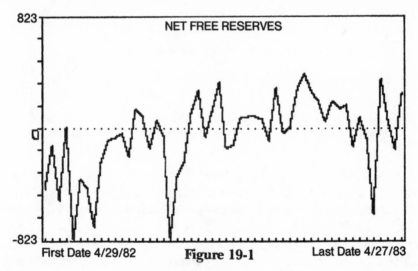

First Date 4/29/82   **Figure 19-1**   Last Date 4/27/83

When net free reserves are negative, the banking system is termed to be in a "net borrowed reserves" position. This means that money is tight and that the necessary funds to fuel a business expansion are not present in the banking system. Such conditions often presage market declines. Conversely, a net free reserves position by the banking system is usually followed by a rising stock market. Even more reliability can be given to the forecast when free reserves are expanding.

MONEY SUPPLY. Another measure of liquidity is the money supply itself. At Weiss Research, our econometric model of the economy shows that the percent change of money-supply growth is a good indicator of future stock-market movements (figure 19-2). Specifically, the percent change in M-1 growth over a 13-week period has a lagged positive correlation with the Standard and Poors 500 Index with the maximum effect of the money supply change being exhibited some four weeks into the future.

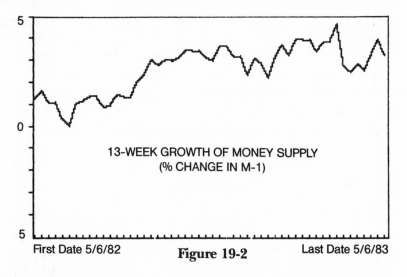

First Date 5/6/82   **Figure 19-2**   Last Date 5/6/83

The **DISCOUNT RATE,** the rate which the Federal Reserve charges its member banks, can often have a dramatic impact on stocks. After a major decline in interest rates (such as the Fed funds rate or T-bill rates) has ended and a rise has begun, a discount-rate hike by the Fed gives the incipient rise in rates an official stamp of approval and can easily set off a major decline in stocks. Conversely, after interest rates have risen dramatically and have begun to decline somewhat, a cut in the discount rate by the Fed is, in effect, their way of telling the market that they intend to pump money into the economy and push rates down, triggering a major stock-market rally.

Thus, as a general rule, a cut in the discount rate can be viewed as bullish for the stock market and an increase in the rate would be considered a negative. Our model has shown the maximum impact on the stock market to be three weeks after a discount-rate change. After a very long interest-rate decline, however, a discount-rate cut can often be viewed as a climactic move. This is especially true if the Fed is trying to artificially lower interest rates by cutting the discount rate well *below* the Federal funds rate—the rate at which banks borrow from each other. The reverse is true after a major rise. In either case, you should be on the lookout for a turnaround in interest rates and, subsequently, in stocks.

FEDERAL FUNDS RATE refers to the rate that banks charge one another for overnight loans and is the most reliable tool for anticipating discount-rate changes. Banks in general have two sources available for borrowing: (1) from the Federal Reserve at the discount rate and (2) from other banks at the "fed funds rate." As a rule, banks prefer to borrow in the overnight "fed funds" market. But when the fed funds rate moves substantially higher than the discount rate, it will generally encourage them to seek more money from the Fed. This can be accurately viewed as having negative connotations for the stock market in that a discount rate hike could be triggered when the Fed Funds rate rises above the discount rate by one percentage point (100 basis points) or more as shown in figure 19-3.

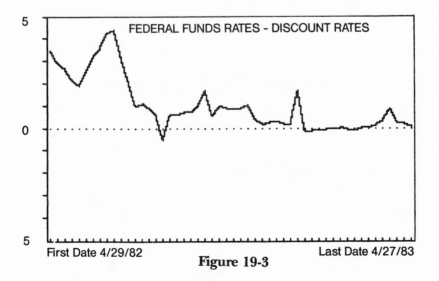

Figure 19-3

These monetary indicators and the various other technical tools described here should help you to determine the general direction of the markets over the medium-term. But in order to further fine-tune your timing, the short-term market indicators may also come in handy as you will see in the next chapter.

20

SHORT-TERM MARKET INDICATORS

With market volatility greater than ever before and with greater leverage available than in most past periods, short-term indicators have become more important in order to give you advance warning of sudden turns.

The **SHORT-TERM TRADING INDEX**, also know as TRIN, evaluates buying and selling pressure. Specifically, it measures the amount of volume going into advancing stocks versus the amount of volume going into declining issues and TRIN can be monitored on a daily or intraday basis. The formula is:

$$TRIN = \frac{(\# \text{ of advancing issues}/\# \text{ of declining issues})}{(\text{upside volume}/\text{downside volume})}$$

As an example, assume that on one day on the New York Stock Exchange we have:

	Issues (number)	Volume (millions of shares)
Advancing	800	50
Declining	600	25

The TRIN that day would be equal to:

$$TRIN = \frac{(800/600)}{(50/25)} = \frac{1.33}{2.0} = .67$$

In this case, buying pressure was stronger than selling pressure as comparatively more volume was going into advancing issues. It is generally accepted that a TRIN of between .65 and .90 is a bullish sign for the short term, while a reading of below .65 is considered *very* bullish. Readings of .90 to 1.10 are regarded as neutral, while TRIN above 1.10 carries bearish connotations.

TRIN can be very helpful in timing your purchases and sales, allowing you to get the very best possible executions of your trades. This can sometimes be crucial, especially when dealing in the options market. For example, if I am planning to sell and TRIN is bullish, I am likely to place my "ask" (sell order) slightly above the current "bid." On the other hand, if TRIN is bearish, I usually place my orders to sell immediately or "at the market" as it is unlikely I will receive a better price by waiting.

Still another way to use TRIN is as a short-term confirmation or non-confirmation of the market averages. In other words, if the market declines one day while TRIN is registering a bullish reading, the chances are that the market decline will not continue. Such divergence over two or three days can often forewarn of a market bottom. Confirmation, on the other hand, would be implied when the market moves up and the TRIN is bullish. In such a case, we would expect still higher prices—at least in the near term.

The Short-Term Trading Index is also sometimes employed as an overbought/oversold indicator by using its 10-day moving average:

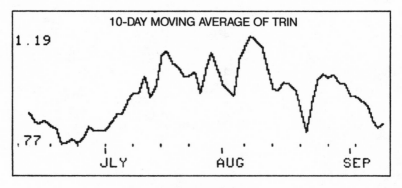

Figure 20-1

If the 10-day moving average of TRIN is below .75, the market is considered to be overbought. If, in addition, the previous one-day reading exceeds 1.20, an immediate correction can be expected.

Conversely, if the 10-day moving average of TRIN is above 1.20, the market is considered to be oversold; and if, in addition, the previous one-day reading is below .65, an immediate corrective rally is called for.

THE TICK indicator is another very commonly cited short-term barometer used intraday since it is updated every few minutes. It refers to the net upticks at that point in time, and can be best described as a snapshot taken of the market which "freezes" the action on the New York Stock Exchange. Each stock whose last trade is completed at a higher price than the previous trade is considered an "uptick." Each stock whose last trade is completed at a lower price is counted as a "downtick." The Tick indicator simply equals all upticks minus all downticks. If traders are bidding prices up, it will be recorded as a higher tick reading. Any reading above + 100 is considered bullish, anything between - 100 and + 100 is neutral, and below -100 is bearish. Thus, the Tick is probably the most sensitive of all market indicators; and by watching *both* the Tick and TRIN you can develop a very good feel for the immediate market direction, timing your purchases and sales accordingly.

21

INDUSTRY GROUPS

Most stocks can be classified according to groups—General Motors, Ford and Chrysler in the automobile group; ASA and HOMESTAKE in the goldmining group, etc. Since most companies within a group tend to move in unison, monitoring their performance can be helpful in various ways: By charting the performance of each group, you can quickly see which ones are leading an advance and which are lagging behind. If you intend to buy particular stocks, the information can make the selection process much easier. Needless to say, it is usually better to buy those issues which are members of an industry group which is leading the market move.

RELATIVE STRENGTH tracks industry groups in comparison to the market as a whole. The performance of each group is compared individually to the performance of the New York Stock Exchange Composite Index over a selected period of time, allowing you to analyze whether it is outperforming or underperforming the general market. A ranking can then be assigned to each industry group in terms of its relative strength.

We have developed three methods which will allow you to monitor the performance of the industry groups, using *Barron's* "Industry Stock Groups" for your data.

The first approach plots a chart for a specified industry group showing its performance over the most recent one-year period. This allows you to easily monitor the trend of the group itself as illustrated by the example in figure 21-1.

The second approach studies the group's performance *relative* to the New York Stock Exchange Composite Index during the same period.

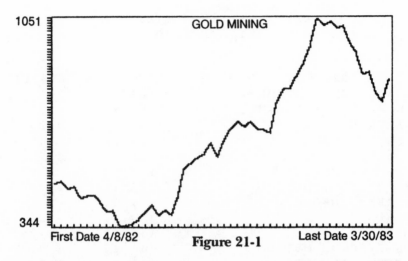

1051

GOLD MINING

344

First Date 4/8/82   **Figure 21-1**   Last Date 3/30/83

These data can add greatly to your information. For example, while the results of approach #1 may show the index of a particular group gaining in price, the results of approach #2 might show the group to actually be lagging behind the market as a whole. On the other hand, the particular group may be seen to be in a downtrend, while examination of the relative strength chart shows that the group is still performing relatively better than the market as a whole.

Finally, when you are looking for short-sale targets, this indicator will alert you to which industries are the weakest.

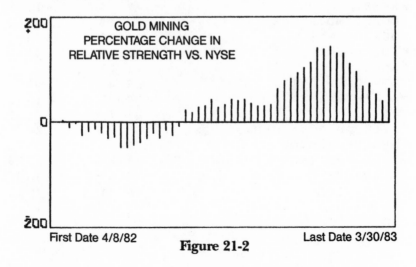

200

GOLD MINING
PERCENTAGE CHANGE IN
RELATIVE STRENGTH VS. NYSE

0

200

First Date 4/8/82   **Figure 21-2**   Last Date 3/30/83

GROUP RELATIVE STRENGTH
PERIOD 1 YEAR

STOCK GROUP	RELATIVE STRENGTH	NET CHANGE
RETAIL MERCHANDISE	183.19	.08
AIRCRAFT MANUFACTURING	155.33	1.83
AIR TRANSPORT	143.65	8.23
GOLD MINING	139.28	9.68
PACKING	133.58	2.7
AUTOMOBILES	127.23	-3.47
OFFICE EQUIPMENT	123.01	1.76
GROCERY CHAINS	119.41	-6.15
RUBBER	119.36	-.01
TEXTILES	117.77	-2.35
NON-FERROUS METALS	115.63	2.45
MOTION PICTURES	112.93	5.7
DOW-JONES TRANSPORTATION	112.32	-.08
ELECTRICAL EQUIPMENT	110.99	-1.54
LIQUOR	107.58	-1.85
MACHINE TOOLS	104.63	4.29
INSTALLMENT FINANCING	103.89	-.05
CHEMICALS	103.82	-1.54
BLDG MATERIALS & EQUIPMENT	102.89	-2.38
DOW-JONES COMPOSITE	102.22	-.55
DOW-JONES INDUSTRIALS	101.89	-.94
DRUGS	101.14	-.12
AUTOMOBILE EQUIPMENT	100.53	-.04
PAPER	97.29	-1.09
FOODS AND BEVERAGES	97.18	-1.61
TOBACCO	96.32	.35
CLOSED-END INVESTMENTS	93.63	.01
BANKS	92.33	1.1
DOW-JONES UTILITIES	84.87	.02
MACHINERY(HEAVY)	84.37	.14
OIL	81.3	-2.58
RAILROAD EQUIPMENT	80.95	.24
FARM EQUIPMENT	79.28	-.98
STEEL AND IRON	78.62	-1.78
INSURANCE	75.45	-1.07
TELEVISION	46.01	-1.22

Figure 21-3

Figure 21-2 is an example of the results of approach #2. Since it is in the form of an oscillator, the industry index may oscillate above or below the center line which represents the New York Stock Exchange Composite Index.

The third approach ranks each industry in terms of relative strength. A rating of 100.00 would mean that the industry performance matched exactly that of the New York Stock Exchange Composite Index during the given period. A net-change figure is also produced denoting the change from last week's reading. Whereas the charts from approach #2 give a historical perspective, the report generated from approach #3 gives a relative strength "snapshot" showing at a glance the strongest industry groups in the *present* (Figure 21-3).

22

STOCK OPTIONS

Some of you who are reading this book may already have a good understanding of stock options and how to use puts and calls in your trading. Others, who might have computer skills, may not have been exposed elsewhere to the elements of option trading. Therefore, in fairness to those unfamiliar with the nomenclature, I will take the next few pages to introduce the reader to the basics. Again, if you are learned in this area, feel free to skip ahead to option strategies at the end of this chapter.

Stock options can be attractive as they offer investors a potentially large profit from a relatively small investment with a known and predetermined risk. The option buyer knows in advance that the most he can lose is the price he has paid for the option. There are two basic types of stock options—*puts and calls*. Let's start with calls.

A CALL is the right to buy 100 shares of a certain stock at a stated price within a given period of time. Common stocks on which options are traded at the Chicago Board Options Exchange (CBOE) include such well known companies as Dow Chemical, IBM, General Motors, Eastman Kodak, etc. In all, it is possible to buy or sell (write) options on approximately 85 different common stocks on the CBOE. The buyer of the option pays to the "writer" (seller) of the option a sum of money which is kept by the writer whether the option is executed or not. This is known as the "premium."

Let's take, as an example, an "April 50 call" on ABC Company. This entitles the buyer to purchase 100 shares of ABC Company at $50 a share any time between now and April.

In the case of CBOE options, each option is normally for 100 shares of a specific, widely held, actively traded security. In the example above, ABC stock is known as the "underlying security." The $50 price at which the option buyer may elect to exercise the option is known as the "exercise price" or "striking price."

"The expiration date" is the last day on which the buyer is entitled to exercise his option to purchase or sell the stock. CBOE options expire quarterly on either a January/April/July/October cycle, or quarterly cycles beginning in February or March. All options actually expire on the Saturday following the third Friday of the expiration date.

A PUT gives you the right to sell short a particular stock at a fixed price. Thus, an ABC Company April 50 put entitles the buyer to sell short 100 shares of ABC Company common stocks at $50 a share any time during the life of the option.

COST OF OPTIONS. How much does it cost to buy an option? The premium varies with each stock and can be affected by several factors:

(1) *The time factor.* Options are termed "wasting" assets. If an option cannot be exercised at a profit by its expiration date, it becomes worthless. Thus, as the expiration date is approached, the option's time value decreases. All else being equal, the more time remaining until the expiration date, the higher the premium will be. For example, an October option for a particular stock normally commands a higher premium than an otherwise identical July option because the buyer of the October option has an additional three months for the underlying stock to move in the direction expected.

(2) *The current market price of the stock in relation to the strike price of the option.* Assume that in January an investor purchases a July 50 call of ABC Company when the price of the stock is also at $50. In such a case, the investor is only paying "for the time value" of the option. But, if by March the price of the stock has risen to $60, a new investor would have to pay a higher premium for the same call than the original investor. With the stock price at $60, the July 50 call is now called an "in-the-money" option because the market price of the stock is greater than the strike price of the call. If exercised immediately, it should yield a profit of roughly $10. Conversely, if the price of the stock

were now $45 instead of $60, the July 50 call would be referred to as "out of the money" since the price of the stock is below the strike price.

(3) *Supply and demand.* Let's assume that numerous investors expect the price of the stock to rise and rush to buy calls rather than the actual stock. This automatically causes the premium to increase in value. Therefore, the price of the option is also a reflection of supply and demand for the options themselves. If the stock has been going up, there will probably be an increased demand for call options on the stock, thus making the premiums more expensive. Remember too, in such a market there is less interest in selling or writing calls by those who own the underlying stock. On the other hand, when the price of the stock is rising, put options are in less demand and are therefore comparatively less expensive.

(4) *The volatility of the underlying stock.* If a particular stock traditionally fluctuates a good deal, its option is likely to command a higher premium than the option for a stock that normally trades in a narrow price range. One common measure of a market's volatility is referred to as its "Beta." Beta is a measure of the average percentage change in the price of a stock relative to the percentage change of a market index. Thus, options on stocks with a higher beta tend to cost more. It is often for this reason that, as a general rule, premiums do not necessarily increase or decrease point for point with the price of the underlying stock. A one point change in the stock price can often result in less than a one point change in the option premium. However, once an option reaches "parity," the premium is likely to move point for point with the stock. (For a call, parity occurs when the exercise price plus the premium equals the market price of the stock. For a put, parity occurs when the exercise price minus the premium equals the market price of the stock.)

Option Strategies

The options market is made up of two different types of players. The first type uses the options market to reduce risk. This type—the investor or "hedger"—usually owns the underlying security; and to insure a known rate of return on his investments, writes (sells) a call against his stock. By doing so, he relinquishes the right to profit from any advance in the value of the stock during the term of the option, in return for the money he will receive from selling the call. If he feels strongly that the price of the stock may decline over the near term, he may purchase a put.

The second type—the speculator—does not usually own the underlying security and thus is termed "naked" when he buys puts or calls. He hopes to profit from a good percentage move in the value of a stock during a short period of time. Making this type of determination is much more difficult than it seems. The odds are stacked heavily against this player.

Option strategies can be extremely complex and, for the most part, are beyond the scope of this book. One good book on the subject is Max Ansbacher's *The New Options Market*, Walker & Company, 720 Fifth Avenue, New York, NY. It would also be a good idea to purchase an "Option Valuation Program," many of which are based on the "Black-Scholes Model" and are available for your personal computer. These programs attempt to evaluate a "fair price" for a given option based on the underlying stock's price and volatility.

Here are a few "general rules" to use in option trading:

1) First, make a decision on the underlying stock before looking at its options.

2) Be sure the stock has a high volatility factor (Beta).

3) Select an option that offers good liquidity—in other words with a volume of at least 500 or so per day.

4) Select an option that is fairly priced.

5) As a rule, select an option that is not too much "out of the money" nor too much "in the money." Usually an option that is "at the money" or slightly "out of the money" is the best choice.

6) Attempt to buy calls on temporary weakness in the stock; and puts, on temporary strength.

7) Usually it is worth the extra cost of the premium to select an option with approximately six months remaining rather than choosing the nearest option.

8) Because the time value of an option declines rapidly as it approaches its expiration date, generally it is wise to either liquidate the option or "roll forward" (sell your option and buy another three to six months forward) when there is two to four weeks remaining before expiration date. And, if you can, the ideal time to take profits is within the first half of the option's life.

IV

CYCLES

23

THE MEANING OF CYCLES

Why do market cycles exist? Could it be that subatomic waves or celestial rotations somehow impact economic behavior? Or do they have a more mundane reason relating to yearly tax planning, harvest cycles, short and long-term business cycles, etc.?

Regardless of the underlying forces, our approach here is merely to accept the fact that cycles do exist in markets—for whatever reason—and to use the data empirically to improve our trading results. Cycle frequencies have been found ranging from just a few minutes to thousands of years, with countless cycles within those extremes. The key, therefore, to using cycles is to determine the *frequency* of the most critical cycles, while keeping in mind shorter and longer-term cycles as well. You would use the *critical* cycles for most of your trading decisions. The shorter-term cycles would aid you in refining your timing of entry and exit points; while the longer-term cycles help you determine the overall market trend.

Because one gains perspective from an understanding of long-term cycles, We wish to acquaint you with three very long-term cycles. A 2000-year "cycle of ages" has been identified within which exists the somewhat better-known 510-year "civilization cycle."

510-Year Civilization Cycle

The 510-year cycle was discovered nearly 40 years ago by Dr. Raymond H. Wheeler, Chairman of the Psychology Department at the University of Kansas. Under his direction, more than 200 researchers worked for over twenty years, studying the influences of weather on mankind. Over 3000 years of weather were evaluated along with nearly two million pieces of weather information. Over 20,000 pieces of art were studied, as was literature throughout history. In excess of 18,000 battles were examined. No stone was left unturned.

After this exhaustive research, Dr. Wheeler concluded that the present 510-year cycle would bottom in the 1980s. He expected the "death of the world" to last until the year 2000. It was his conclusion that at the end of the 510-year cycle is when governments break down and nations collapse, and that there is a wave of international wars which are "nation-falling wars." He also expected "the initiative to pass from West to East for the next 510-year period."

170-Year Drought Cycle

Within the 510-year civilization cycle are three 170-year drought cycles, verified by the ring structure of 3000-year-old redwood trees. A number of rings very close together indicates a period of drought; a series of rings further apart indicates a time of good moisture. These have tended to group into both 50-year and 170-year cycles.

At the end of a 170-year cycle, the climate turns cold and there are significant droughts. One man who has done a great deal of study on the 170-year and the 510-year cycles is R. E. McMaster, publisher of *The Reaper* (P. O. Box 39026, Phoenix, AZ 85069). He believes the 170-year cycle is also bottoming. He states: "It looks as if we are just going into one of those cold, dry cycles. The unexpected eruptions of Mt. St. Helens and El Chinchond in Mexico have added to the cooling of the climate by the debris that they have placed in the air. This and other predicted climatic changes could affect our food supply."

Kondratieff Cycle (50-54 Years)

Kondratieff, a Russian economist, based his study primarily on statistical data including wholesale prices, interest rates, wage levels, and indexes of production for the period 1780 to 1920, using the United States, Great Britain, France and Germany as the primary models. His conclusions, presented in a 1925 paper entitled *The Long Waves In Economic Life*, were basically that the existence of a cycle of from 48 to 60 years in the overall economic activity of the Western world was highly probable. These preliminary conclusions have since been reinforced by the more extensive work of Joseph Schumpeter, Edward R. Dewey and others who have concluded the ideal length of the cycle to be 54 years.

Historians tell us that this "half-century" business cycle has actually been in existence thousands of years. In the Old Testament, the land was to lie fallow every seventh year; and after seven groups of these seven years—a total of 49 years—the land was to lie fallow two years in a row. More importantly, it was in this fiftieth year, the Year of Jubilee, that all debts were to be cancelled, all indentured servants set free, and all land reverted back to the original owners—a classical "housecleaning process."

At the beginning of the fifty-year biblical cycle, long-term borrowing would be common, but as the cycle began to draw to a close, money would only be available for a few years, until the forty-ninth year when only one-year loans were available. This also created a real estate cycle. If you bought some land at the very beginning of the cycle, the value was high because you could use it for fifty years; and forty years into the cycle, prices would supposedly be much lower because you could only use it for ten years before the title reverted to the original owner.

The pressing question today is: *Where are we now in the Kondratieff cycle?* Most economists, still hoping for many more years of uninterrupted prosperity, will deny the validity of long waves; but among those analysts that accept it—although there are differences of opinion as to the exact date of the peak—there is near unanimous agreement that it occurred in the 1970s and that we are now in the decline phase. The idealized peaks have been identified as occurring in 1814, 1864, 1920 and 1973.

Richard Zambell, the Director of Economic Research at our firm, Weiss Research, Inc., demonstrates that although the *absolute level* of economic activity has continued to rise, in terms of the *rate* of real GNP growth rates, the approximate peak was indeed in 1973. Moreover, his large-scale econometric model of the economy is unique in that it is probably the first to use this concept as one of its underlying assumptions.

Because cycles are never exact, however, it is more appropriate to look at this cycle in terms of its broad phases, which can be divided roughly into five decades:

First Decade	--	Recovery
Second Decade	--	Boom
Third Decade	--	Peak and Transition
Fourth Decade	--	Collapse
Fifth Decade	--	Trough and Transition

From this perspective, we must also conclude that the 1980s represent the fourth decade in this cycle. One of the leading experts on the Kondratieff Wave is Don Hoppe, publisher of The Donald J. Hoppe Analysis (P. O. Box 977, Crystal Lake, IL 60014). Another newsletter publisher who is deeply committed to this field of research is Jim McKeever, *The McKeever Strategy Letter* (P. O. Box 4130, Medford, OR 97501).

24

HISTORICAL STOCK-MARKET CYCLES

Just as business cycles have been shown to exist in the economy, so too have cycles been identified in the stock market. But, although their existence is generally agreed upon, the determination of when they will peak or bottom is often the subject of debate. This chapter will introduce you to some of the better research that has been undertaken in the field.

The following work on historical stock-market cycles was taken from Edward R. Dewey's classic *Cycles*. This is known as the bible for anyone interested in cycle behavior and is published by the Foundation for the Study of Cycles in Philadelphia.

THE 9.2-YEAR CYCLE in the stock market is well documented back to the 1830s; and it was calculated that there is only one chance out of 5000 that these occurrences could have been coincidental. Interestingly, this same 9.2-year cycle was documented elsewhere in nature 37 different times. To be completely accurate on the average, the cycle measured exactly 9.225 years. The base year was calculated as 1832.5 and the ideal crests were timed at 3.76753 years after such cycle bottoms.

According to Dewey, the cause of the 9.2-year cycle in stock prices must be sought outside of the market itself because many other completely unrelated phenomena display cycles of this same period with crests or turning points coming at almost exactly the same time. Some such unrelated phenomena which he cited are sunspot activity, the abundance of grasshoppers and tree rings. He felt that there may be one or more environmental forces with periods at or very close to this length, and that these forces may trigger responses on the part of the various phenomena.

THE 18.2-YEAR CYCLE in the stock market is well documented but not quite as consistent as the 9.2-year cycle. It was calculated that there is only a one-in-twenty chance that this cycle could be the result of coincidence. Based on data through 1964, the following crests and troughs were found:

TABLE 24-1. 18.2-YEAR CYCLE – ACTUAL

Crest	Trough
1835	1842
1852	1859
1868	1877
1881	1897
1905	1921
1929	1932
1936	1942
1961	

The data of the idealized crests, the actual crests and the differences are shown below:

TABLE 24-2. 18.2-YEAR CYCLE – IDEALIZED

Ideal Crest	Actual Crest	Difference
1833.6	1835.5	+1.9
1851.8	1852.5	+0.7
1870.0	1868.5	-1.5
1882.2	1887.5	+5.3
1906.4	1905.5	-0.9
1924.6	1929.5	+4.9
1942.8	1936.5	-6.3
1961.0	1961.5	+0.5

THE 46-MONTH CYCLE was discovered by Veryl L. Dunbar in 1947 and was later discussed by him in an article called "The Bull Market" which was printed in *Barron's* in June of 1952. The cycle had come true 62 out of 64 times during the past 123 years at the time the article was written, showing an accuracy of 97%. He stated: "In only two instances did the stock index fail to reach a higher level in the year in which the top of the cycle was reached than in the preceding low year of the cycle. Unusually remarkable, however, is the fact that the index was lower in every instance in the year in which the bottom of this cycle was reached than it was in the preceding crest year of the cycle."

Contrary to the usual conception of cycles, the apex does not fall equidistant between two lows, but instead occurs in the year immediately preceding a low. Also, the 46 month cycle seems to be "M" shaped.

The shape might possibly be accounted for by cycles 23 months in length, and perhaps 15 1/3 months in length. Regardless, Dunbar states that the cycle bottom usually occurs one year after the cycle top, suggesting that you should be long three years and short one year.

Dunbar believes that over longer periods of time, the cycles recur at intervals of 3-4-4-4-4-4 years and then repeat with six cycles recurring in a period of approximately 23 years, twelve in 46 years, etc. He also has observed similar rhythms of 23 years and 46 years in other phenomena.

THE 41-MONTH CYCLE is said to have been present in industrial common stock prices from their beginning in 1871. Its average length has been 40.7 months or 3.39 years. The cycle was first observed in 1912 and was secretly used by a group to successfully trade the market during World War I. Some ten years later in 1923, a similar cycle was discovered in commercial paper rates by Professor W. L. Crum of Harvard. At the same time, Professor Joseph Kitchin, also of Harvard, discovered a 40-month cycle existing in six different economic time series.

The original 41-month stock market cycle was later rediscovered in 1935 by Chapin Hoskins of New York, who knew nothing of the earlier work.

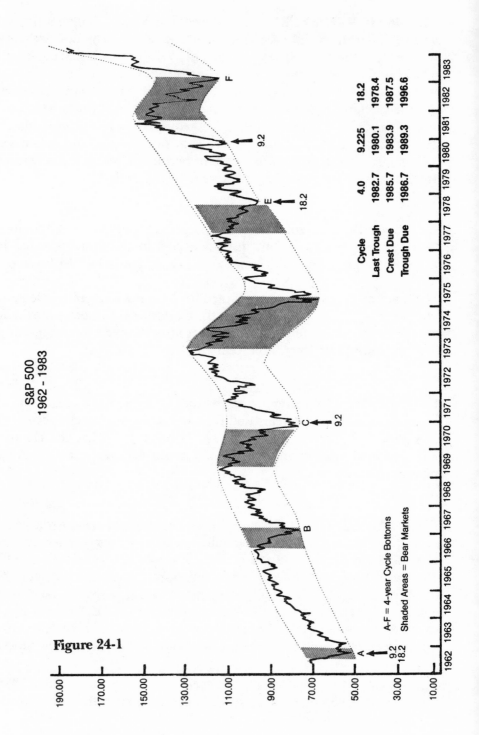

Figure 24-1

S&P 500
1962 - 1983

A-F = 4-year Cycle Bottoms

Shaded Areas = Bear Markets

Cycle	4.0	9.225	18.2
Last Trough	1982.7	1980.1	1978.4
Crest Due	1985.7	1983.9	1987.5
Trough Due	1986.7	1989.3	1996.6

Dewey points out that the existence of these cycles means that important highs followed by important lows tend to succeed each other with a beat and at intervals which average this length. However, it should not be misconstrued that they will succeed each other at the precise length of the cycle, in that some turning points are early and some are late.

In Figure 24-1, we have attempted to update some of this research on historical stock-market cycles. Currently, the three most dominant cycles in the stock market are the 18.2-year cycle, 9.225-year cycle and the 4.0-year cycle (discussed more thoroughly in the next chapter). Other interpretations of the timing of these cycles may be as valid as ours; only time will tell.

JOHN HURST, a pioneer in stock-market cycle work in the late 1960s, identified 12 dominant cycles existing in the stock market. These still exist today, though the duration may have changed slightly (see following table).

TABLE 24-3.   DOMINANT STOCK MARKET CYCLES

Years	Months	Weeks
18		
9		
4.5		
3.0		
1.5	18	
1.0	12	
.75	9	
* .50	6	26
* .25	3	13
	1.5	6.5
	.75	3.25
	.375	1.625

* The 26 and 13-week cycles may also be viewed as combining to form what is, in effect, an 18-week nominal cycle.

JOHN M. COOPER, in later works, identified the low points of the 50-month cycle (Hurst's 4.5 year cycle) and also the 18-month cycle:

TABLE 24-4.   50 MONTH CYCLE

Trough-to-Trough Dates	Duration

1855-1921:	
Jan. 1885 - June 1888	41
June 1888 - Dec. 1890	30
Dec. 1890 - Aug. 1893	32
Aug. 1893 - Aug. 1896	36
Aug. 1896 - Sept. 1900	49
Sept. 1900 - Sept. 1903	36
Sept. 1903 - Nov. 1907	50
Nov. 1907 - July 1910	32
July 1910 - Dec. 1914	53
Dec. 1914 - Dec. 1917	36
Dec. 1917 - Aug. 1921	<u>44</u>
Average	40

NOTE: Between 1885 and 1921, this cycle averaged 40 months in length.

1934 - 1974:	
July 1934 - March 1938	44
March 1938 - April 1942	49
April 1942 - Oct. 1946	54
Oct. 1946 - June 1949	32
June 1949 - Sept. 1953	51
Sept. 1953 - Oct. 1957	49
Oct. 1957 - June 1962	56
June 1962 - Oct. 1966	51
Oct. 1966 - May 1970	44
May 1970 - Dec. 1974	<u>55</u>
Average	50

Thus, we have seen what has been done with cycles in the past. Our next step is to try to apply these same methods to the present.

25

PRACTICAL USE OF CYCLES

A solid knowledge of cycles can keep you on the right side of a major trend and also give you a pretty good idea of when that trend may reverse.

For the "buy-and-hold" stock market investor, a familiarity with long-term cycles—especially the 4-year stock-market cycle—is usually adequate. But the more astute and active stock market traders realize that considerably more money can be made from shorter-term market fluctuations by alternately shifting from the long to the short side of the market. Such an approach, of course, demands more time and effort. What most people don't realize, however, is that the results which can be obtained via short-term trading are potentially phenomenal.

Compare this hypothetical example of *trading versus investing*. Let's say you purchase $10,000 of XYZ stock. The stock does well and by the end of the year, you have a 75% profit of $7,500. Your friend, meanwhile, decides to trade several different stocks, making on average one trade per month, yielding an average profit of 10%, resulting in a total profit of $31,380 or 313% per year. Why the incredible difference? The answer is *compounding*. After each trade, he was able to reinvest the entire proceeds, allowing compounding to work for him. To make it work, however, you have to (1) trade short-term so as to maximize your percent yield per period of time and (2) stay fully invested at all times.

It sounds good in theory, but does it work? The answer is yes—if your *timing and selection* are good. You must select stocks that offer a high probability of moving up or down by a good percentage in a short period of time. After you have selected a stock, you must buy it just as it begins to move. You must also have an objective of what price you expect the stock to reach and in what period of time. Then, when the stock has reached that objective, you must sell it and immediately buy another stock from among the candidates you are tracking that meet your criteria.

Short-term cycles are crucial. By identifying specific cycles for specific stocks, you can learn to predict how prices will be affected – not only in terms of the direction they will move, but also in terms of the speed and the extent of such a move.

Why do stock prices move? It is commonly believed that roughly 75% of stock-price movement occurs as a result of foreseeable, fundamental events influencing investor thinking. This causes the long-term trend. Unforeseen fundamental events add a random element to the market and account for approximately 2% of price movement. *The remaining 23% can be attributed to the influence of cyclic forces*—a large enough influence to allow us to construct short-term trades that take advantage of this movement.

The *duration* or *period* of a cycle is the horizontal measure from trough to trough. The *magnitude* is the vertical measure from peak to trough. Generally, cycles of longer duration exhibit greater magnitude. Cycles may also be summed together to create other cycles.

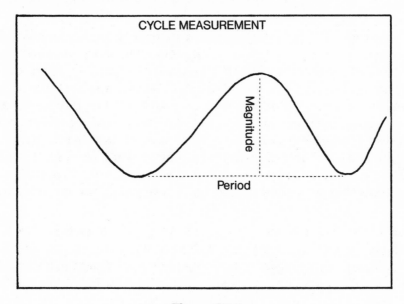

Figure 25-1

A good place to start locating and identifying cycles is in the stock market as a whole. Each stock does have its own cyclicality. But often it is very similar to the overall market. (See previous chapter for examples on how this has been done in the past.)

The next step is to take a chart of the stock market or a particular issue and, moving backwards in time, attempt to identify bottoms. You should find six or seven reasonably distinct bottoms. Measure the distance (in days or weeks) between each one and then simply calculate the average length of your cycle. A typical example might be cycles of 18, 15, 16, 14, 20 and 17 days or an average 100 / 6 = 16.67 days.

In order to project when the cycle will bottom again, we allow for ten percent error in either direction (.10 x 16.67 = 1.67), adding this value to the average or ideal length to find the maximum days in which the cycle can be expected to bottom (16.67 + 1.67 = 18.34), and subtracting it to determine the minimum (16.67 - 1.67 = 15). Thus, we can project—with some degree of certainty—that the price will bottom between 15 and 19 days after our last identified bottom.

By adding this time dimension to our analysis techniques we have now taken a quantum leap forward in market strategy. Suppose we have picked out a stock that we wish to purchase. We believe it is in a strong bull market and have identified a 15 - 19 day cycle. Furthermore, we have determined that the last cycle bottom occurred 12 days ago. Because of our cycle analysis, we can expect the market to move lower until the cycle bottom occurs three to seven days from now. By waiting a few days we will not only be able to buy the stock at a better price but will have reasonable expectations of a swing upwards from then on.

Enveloping

Another technique we can use to help us with cyclic analysis is called "enveloping." The object is to draw a curved channel or envelope around prices, connecting successive lows and successive highs, keeping the channel between them at a constant width. Later, you can then draw a tighter channel within the original channel or a larger channel around it. These envelopes will help you to identify cycle bottoms, to visually see the general direction of the market and to set price objectives by projecting your channels several weeks ahead. Remember, prices are *generally more likely* to remain within the channel boundaries you have projected than to break out of them, but this is no guarantee they will hold in defiance of other indicators:

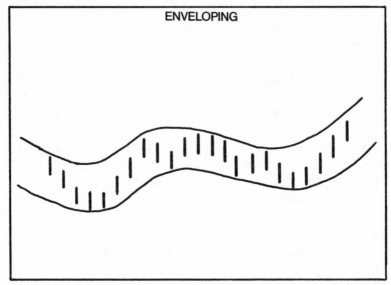

ENVELOPING

Figure 25-2

In earlier chapters we spent a lot of time learning about chart patterns. We learned how to identify the Double Top, Head and Shoulders, Triangle, etc. and how to use them to our advantage. We can tilt the odds in our favor by employing these patterns because they "tend" to resolve themselves in a certain manner. But sometimes the patterns abort, crumble or simply don't work.

Chartists rarely know why a pattern fails or why a pattern is successful. Most don't care to know. But the fact is that, to a large degree, chart patterns are the result of a combination of cyclic forces interacting on the price of a stock. Nearly every chart pattern, when broken down to its basic elements, contains: (1) a trend component; (2) a short-term cycle component; and (3) a longer-term cycle component. Figure 25-3 shows an example of what those components might look like separately, as well as when combined.

Voila! We have created a Head and Shoulders pattern. We have demonstrated how it can be formed as a result of the combination of

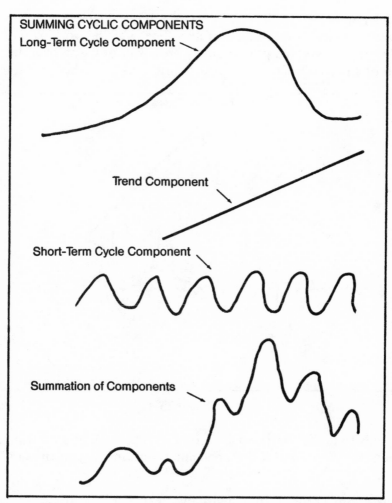

Figure 25-3

cyclic and trend components. The chartist looks for a break of the neckline to confirm that the trend has turned down. The cycle analyst realizes the trend is turning down because the longer-term cycle is topping out and will be moving down for quite some time. They are both looking at the same price pattern and are forming similar conclusions.

The chartist has learned empirically, from examination of hundreds of charts, that a break of the neckline will usually be followed by a major downward move. He must act strictly on probabilities. We feel that the cycle analyst, by understanding the reason behind price movement, has an advantage. You will see why by examining figure 25-4. After an up move, a typical triangle has formed. The chartist, working with probabilities, knows that prices usually break out of triangles in the direction of the trend. Thus, he expects prices to go higher and soon.

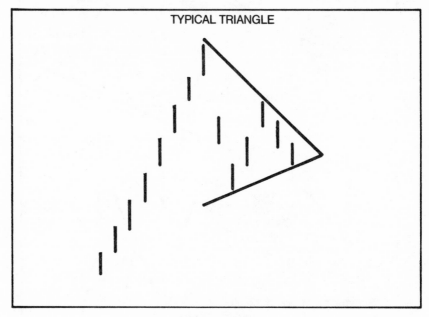

TYPICAL TRIANGLE

Figure 25-4

But this time the chartist will be fooled. The cycle analyst will realize that a major cycle has just topped and is now moving down as in figure 25-5.

Look at any graph. Can you visually "detrend" the graph—weed out the trend to examine the cycle? Or, can you "decycle" the graph in order to examine just the trend? Probably not. But fortunately your computer can do it for you.

First we will use our computer to find the trends and then to *weed out* those trends, leaving us the cycles.

Finding Trends

Moving averages can help us to view longer-term cycles (which is, in effect, the long-term trend) more clearly by eliminating the presence of shorter-term cycles. For example, a 10-week moving average will

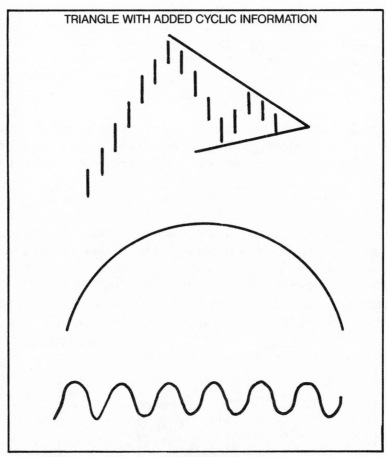

Figure 25-5

eliminate the presence of any cycles 10 weeks or less in duration. By choosing the span of the moving average, you can control which cycles you want to suppress while allowing cycles of longer length to be visible.

Going back to the cycles that we know to exist in the stock market, we can see that a 10-week moving average suppresses the 6.5-week cycle and those smaller, while allowing cycles of 13 weeks or more to come through. A 30-week moving average, commonly used in stock-market forecasting, suppresses the 26-week cycle and those smaller, while allowing the 9-month cycle and those larger to be viewed.

At this time let me alert you to an important caution about moving averages. Many analysts automatically plot the moving average in the slot for the last day of the period. For example, they plot the average for a 10-day period on the 10th day, giving you the impression that the moving average is *lagging* price changes. In cycle work, however, where timing is the main goal, it is best to *center* the moving average, plotting the 10th day between the 5th and 6th day so that stock prices and the average are time coordinated. With this in mind, it might be easier to use an odd number of days so that a stock price can be directly associated with a particular moving average. When you are purchasing a program be sure it allows you the option to plot a "centered" moving average.

A centered moving average also allows you to draw more accurate envelopes. You simply draw in your envelope boundaries at equal distances above and below the moving average line, following the same contour and attempting to find an ideal width that encompasses most tops and bottoms. The centered moving average also makes cycles of smaller duration more visible. As in figure 25-6, they now can be seen to oscillate around the moving average in sympathy with the shortest cycle component that the average does not suppress.

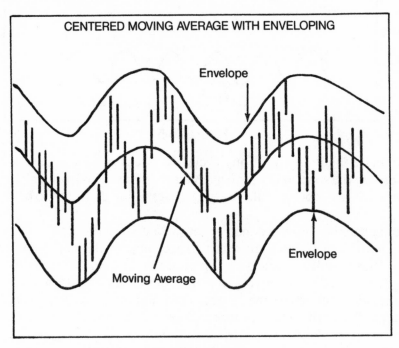

Figure 25-6

Putting the Techniques into Practice

Here are some basic steps you can follow:

Step 1. Browse through a weekly stock or commodity chart book and select those that appear to have good cyclicality.

Step 2. Identify the major bottoms and also draw in your envelope.

Step 3. Build a data file for the issue covering the periods in question.

Step 4. Using a moving average the length of your longest identified cycle, run a centered moving average on the data; and use it to further fine-tune your envelope if necessary.

Step 5. Now try to identify one or two shorter cycles, using one of them to draw in a tighter envelope.

Step 6. Look for *convergence*—a situation in which all three cyclic components will be turning up at nearly the same time. You should get a powerful up move during the time that those cycles are in synch. For example, if you find a 15-week cycle which has just bottomed last week, plus 8-week and 4-week cycles due to bottom in the next week or two, you would have exactly the type of convergence you need to buy a stock.

The technique works equally well in anticipation of a short sale. You identify a market in which the sum of all longer components (in other words, the trend) is down and one or two shorter cycle components are due to top in the near future. A breaking of the uptrend line can help to confirm when those cycles have topped or have started moving down—the ideal time to initiate a short sale.

Figure 25-7 illustrates prices with both a 5-week and 10-week cycle. The square represents your buy zone—the time period when you expect the cycles to bottom and begin moving up. A break in the downtrend line is your signal to buy.

Your transaction is not truly complete until you do one more thing—put in your "stop"—an order which, in this instance, will limit any losses by automatically selling your stocks (or, if you're short, automatically buying it back) should prices start to go against your expectations. Not

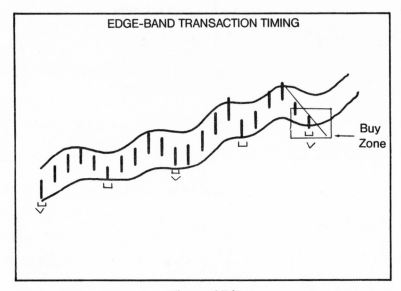

Figure 25-7

all trades can be winners and it is important that you protect your capital by cutting short any erosion you might suffer on losing trades. A safe place for your stop on this trade would be just below the recent cycle bottoms.

Setting Time & Price Objectives

Assuming the stock does move according to expectations, the next question that arises is: Where do we take profits—when it reaches a predetermined price or after a certain amount of time has elapsed? Determining objectives in advance is a necessary part of the strategy. In order for our plan to work we must be able to evaluate risk versus reward on the amount of funds invested. We must also be able to estimate how long it will take for our objective to be reached in order to maximize our profit per *unit of time* invested.

There are several ways to measure objectives. But first you must consider the time factor. Assuming you are trading based on a 10-week cycle and that the summation of all longer cycles is up, you can expect your 10-week cycle to top approximately six to eight weeks after its last bottom. So, this is the time zone when we can expect to sell the stock.

Another way to get a rough idea of where prices might go is to extend your envelope out into the future. Your price envelope was drawn so as to include nearly all price action in the past. So, it is likely that future price action will be contained within the boundaries of your constant-width envelope projected into the future. When prices reach the top of that envelope they are likely to fall, and when they reach the bottom, are likely to rise.

Moving averages can also be used to predict the extent of a price move. You should construct a one-half span moving average. Thus, if you are trading on a 10-week cycle, you would construct and plot a 5-week "centered" moving average. When the 5-week moving average reverses its direction to up, note the price of the stock and how much it has already moved up. You may expect prices to continue to climb until the stock has moved up this much more.

Another method is to:

(1) Use both a one-half span and full-span moving average (both centered).

(2) Project both moving averages up to current time to fill in the missing few days caused by the lag (because they are centered).

(3) At the point where they cross, note the price of the stock and how much it has moved up from its recent bottom. The stock should continue to move that much higher.

(4) Give your objective a plus or minus ten percent tolerance for errors to set up a *target zone.*

Sometimes, although your cyclic analysis shows that prices still have room to move on the upside in terms of time, prices begin moving up strongly but then fall back somewhat forming either a flag or a triangle. This pause in upward price movement offers a good way to predict the extent of the next price move subsequent to the consolidation period. Referring to figure 25-8 follow these steps:

(1) Measure the diagonal distance from Y to Z.

(2) Find the midpoint and mark it with an M.

(3) Measure the vertical distance from M to X.

(4) Add this same distance to M to get your price objective.

(5) If you're trading in a bear market with short sales, follow exactly the same procedure subtracting the distance to M to determine your target.

(6) Set up your target *zone* as in the previous example.

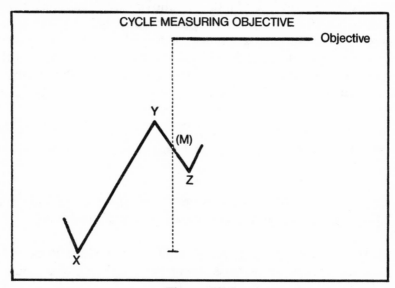

Figure 25-8

Detrending

You have probably been wondering where your computer comes into play in cyclic analysis. We have already covered one area where your computer can save you much time and effort—moving averages. Other techniques such as envelope analysis and projecting objectives can be accomplished via manual, visual and graphic methods. But, when it comes to more sophisticated cyclic analysis such as detrending, use of the computer becomes a must.

Since the price is composed of the summation of a trend component and various cycle components, we can benefit greatly by techniques which separate the two automatically.

In the previous chapter, we found we could better see the trend by eliminating the effect of the shorter term cycles. A moving average of a specific length eliminated the effect of all cycles of that length or less, leaving only the trend and cycles of a longer length present in the data. Conversely if we want to see the cycles more clearly, we can filter out the trend. It is this process which we call "detrending."

It is actually quite simple:

Step 1. Run a moving average on the data. If you select an 11-week moving average, it eliminates the cyclic information of all cycles of eleven weeks or less in length.

Step 2. Subtract the moving average from the actual prices.

Step 3. The result is all price movements *less* the short-term cycles -- ergo the trend. A detrending program can be easily purchased; and Computrac includes one in their package. Figure 25-9 illustrates the process.

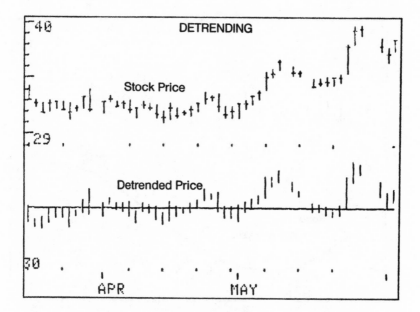

Figure 25-9

FOURIER ANALYSIS is another way to filter out price trends. It refers to various techniques designed to extract as much information as possible from a time series of discrete numbers—including the frequency, amplitude and phase of a series of waves. This method is also called "spectral analysis."

Basically, it separates those fluctuations which have frequencies *below* a certain value from those *above* that value. When we used a moving average to filter out short cycles (high frequencies) and while allowing long cycles (low frequencies) to "pass through" we were using what is called a "lowpass filter." Likewise, when we used the detrending process, allowing only the high frequencies to show through, we were using a "high-pass filter." When a filtering process produces results that lie between two fixed bounds, it is called a "band-pass filter."

Once results have been obtained from spectral analysis, sophisticated curve fitting techniques can be applied to project those results into the future. Explanations of numerical analysis, spectral analysis, filters and curve fitting are beyond the scope of this book. However, should you have a computer, such sophisticated techniques are available to you and are worthy of later investigation:

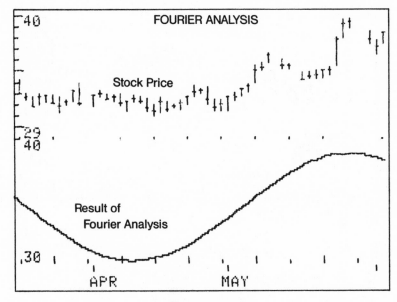

Figure 25-10

Cycle analysis is a massive field in itself. Therefore, in order to help you avoid many hours of time and research on possibly tangential concerns, we've summarized this chapter into 15 basic steps you can follow for limiting losses and maximizing your profits. (Not every step is absolutely necessary for profitable trading. But the more homework you do which produces confirming signals, the greater your margin of certainty.)

1. Begin by trying to identify the presence of cycles in the major averages. For this purpose, you may use the New York Stock Exchange Composite Index, Standard and Poors 500 Index or the Dow Jones Industrial Average.

2. Scan each of the industry groups to determine which are showing relative strength and which are showing relative weakness.

3. Keeping in mind the direction of the averages as well as industry groups, scan the charts of individual issues and select about a half dozen that appear to have a well-defined presence of regular cycles.

4. For each stock, project when the cycle you have identified is due to bottom next, (or in a bear market, due to reach a cyclical top.) To do this, measure the distance between each cycle bottom (or top) and average those cycle lengths. Then add the average length to the last cycle bottom allowing for a ten percent error either way.

5. Envelope each of the stocks to better visualize where each is likely to go.

6. If you have one, run a detrending program to better identify your "trading" cycle and any other smaller cycles that might be present.

7. Run a full-span moving average to suppress your cycle and allow you to clearly see the trend.

8. Run a half-span moving average to give you another technique for projecting an objective.

9. Monitor each of the stocks selected. Ideally, for a good "buy" signal,

both the averages and the industry group should be in uptrends. Your stock should be in an uptrend as indicated by an upward rising line on the fullspan moving average. (Or for a good "sell short" signal, all three should be in downtrends.)

10. After the trading cycle has crested and prices begin moving down, a downtrend line should be drawn. Once prices enter the time zone when the trading cycle is due to bottom, the downtrend line should be watched closely. When prices break up through the downtrend line it is time to buy the stock. Favorable volume patterns would show volume decreasing as the stock dropped in price; then increasing as it moved up through its downtrend line. (Likewise, if you're trading on the short side, the time to sell short is when prices break down through your uptrend line while falling from the cycle top.)

11. Place a stop slightly below the recent cycle bottom (or above the recent top, if you are short).

12. Determine an objective of what price the stock might reach and during what time period, corresponding to the crest of your trading cycle. Be sure to take into account the possible effects of any shorter or longer term cycles on the trading cycle. An objective in price can be gained from (a) envelope projection, (b) full and half-span moving average techniques and (c) the measurement technique presented. If you have time, once you've completed this work, for further confirmation refer back to other techniques for projecting objectives via chart patterns (Double Bottoms, Head and Shoulders Bottoms, Triangles, etc.) Also, take into consideration any overhead resistance that might lessen or stall the upmove.

13. As prices move up, making a series of higher bottoms, move your sell stop up accordingly to lock in profits in the event the unexpected should occur. (And if you're short, bring your buy stop down accordingly.)

14. Once prices have reached your objective in time and price, you can either take profits or you can wait for a break of the trend line to stop you out of the trade.

15. As soon as you have taken profits, repeat the process on another

stock which fits your selection criteria.

These same rules work equally well in the commodity markets. But before you move from the relatively tried and tested world of securities traded mostly in New York City to the whirlwind of futures still dominated by the Chicago markets, you should be fully appraised of the potential risks. Unlike most security trading, in commodities you are responsible for, and you could lose, significantly more than the money you put up for margin.

V

COMMODITY MARKETS

26

GETTING STARTED

The terms "commodity markets" and "futures markets" are often used interchangeably, but are not exactly the same.

Futures markets need not be *only commodities*. They refer to all those markets where the actual purchase of physical goods is to take place at a specified future date. Originally, only agricultural commodities such as soybeans or cattle were traded. But now a wide variety of instruments — foreign currencies, T-bonds and T-bills, and precious metals—have been added.

Likewise, commodity markets need not be limited exclusively to "futures." You can buy and sell soybeans for delivery in future months, or you can buy the actual goods ("physicals") in the "spot" or "cash" markets.

For the purpose of this book, however, we use the term commodity markets to refer to "futures" of any kind and we will use the terms interchangeably.

If you have never traded commodities, I would strongly urge you to devote ample time to learning as much as possible about the subject *before* committing your capital. Most major brokerage houses can provide you with free literature. Your local library should also have books on commodity trading. A good comprehensive book for beginners is *Winning in the Commodity Markets* by George Angell, published by Doubleday. I also recommend a subscription to *Futures Magazine*, 219 Parkade, Cedar Falls, IA 50613. Finally, many valuable free publications are available from the Chicago Board of Trade, Marketing Department, LaSalle at Jackson, Chicago, IL 60604.

Many of you who are reading this book have never traded the futures market. You have probably heard fantastic success stories in which a very small investor parlayed a few thousand dollars into millions within a few short years; or you may have heard horror stories of how people have been literally wiped out of house and home.

Both are most likely true; but in the final analysis, it is the losers that outnumber the winners among the speculators in the futures market. It has been estimated that the typical neophyte trader will only survive three to six months before losing his stake. Yet in the same period of time, a handful out of every 100 or so new players entering the market will have turned a $15,000 stake into several hundred thousand dollars. Granted, the luck of the draw played some part in both the winners' and losers' fate.

One reason you may wish to pursue the commodity markets is because it offers more for the money. *The tools of technical analysis that you have learned in this book apply equally well to both stocks and commodities.* So why not avail yourself of the opportunities in the commodity markets?

A futures transaction is no more than a formalized *contract* or promise to buy or sell a commodity or financial instrument on a specific date. It is this contract—and not the physical goods or securities—which is bought and sold; and in practice, only a very small percentage of buyers or sellers actually receive or deliver physical goods.

Futures markets exist primarily to transfer risk—especially from the commercial participant, or hedger, for whom futures markets were designed – to the speculator. The "commercials" are the firms whose business includes the same or similar commodity or financial instrument as that being traded in the futures market—involving agricultural commodities, forest products, precious and other non-ferrous metals, energy, and money market instruments.

The risk seekers, or speculators, can be divided into two categories of traders. The first category—the locals—consists of a group of professional brokers who trade on the floor for the benefit of their own account. Like the specialists in the stock market, they provide a valuable function to the markets because their frequent trading adds "liquidity"—the ability to buy or sell at any time.

Locals, in turn, can be classified according to their frequency of trading as either "position traders," "day traders," or "scalpers." Position traders may hold a position for days or weeks, while day traders close out their position at the end of each day. Scalpers, on the other hand, may get in and out of the market 50 or more times per day. Because they do not pay commissions, they are willing to trade for very small profits. They may initiate and offset trades literally within seconds and may become bullish or bearish on a commodity's prospects in an equally short period of time.

The other category of speculators are usually termed "commission house traders." The term derives from the fact that the orders come into the pit from outside by way of a brokerage house such as Merrill Lynch. This category could be further subdivided into managed funds and individual speculators.

It is important to understand how a commercial producer of a commodity uses the insurance aspect of the futures market. Suppose a hog breeder expects to bring his animals to market in three months. He knows that at today's price he would have a fair profit. But he has no way of knowing what the price will be three months from now. He may have reason to suspect the possibility that excess supply could lower the price substantially, causing him a loss and possible bankruptcy. Can he afford to take that risk? Obviously not. But he can, in effect, sell his hogs *now* at today's high price by selling short the equivalent number of futures contracts in hogs three months out. He will have essentially locked in today's price and transferred the risk to a speculator. If the price of hogs goes down, he loses money when he sells his hogs but he will make up the difference from his profitable short sale in the futures market. Conversely, if the price of hogs rises, he will lose money in the futures market, while obtaining higher prices at market for his own hogs. Thus, regardless of future price movements, he will be insured or "hedged" against loss.

Why are speculators lured to the futures markets? Simply because of the extreme leverage that is available. Since futures positions are taken on low margin, the trader's gains or losses are magnified. With the margin deposit for a future contract often less than five percent of face value, just a small change in price can result in considerable gains or losses relative to the initial deposit.

To protect against catastrophic losses we would recommend always using stops—the instruction to liquidate your position when a specified price is reached. For example, if you go long (buy) a gold futures contract at $400, you might place a stop at $380 in order to limit your loss in case the market moves down. Conversely, if you sold short a gold futures contract at $500, you might wish to place a protective stop at $520.

Mistakes can be extremely costly in the futures markets. Therefore, it is very important to understand the different types of orders that you can give your broker before you begin trading. Orders can be first classified as either (1) *a day order* which is cancelled if not executed during that day, or (2) *an open order* which remains in effect until cancelled (also referred to as GTC—"good till cancelled"). Orders are assumed to be day orders unless otherwise specified.

In addition, there are four basic trading orders:

(1) *Market order*—one which must be executed by the pit broker as soon as possible after he receives it and at the best obtainable price at that time. Here is an example: "Buy one July silver at the market." In this case, you can be certain to be "filled" (your order executed) at the going price.

(2) *Market-if-touched (MIT) order.* If it's a buy, it becomes a market order as soon as the contract sells or is offered at or *below* the price you have specified; and if it is a sell, it becomes a market order when the contract sells or is bid at or *above* the price you have specified.

(3) *Fixed price order, commonly called a "limit order,"* is an order to buy or sell at a stipulated price. The limit order will be filled as soon as the stipulated price or a price more favorable than the stipulated one can be obtained. Sometimes a limit order can be used to obtain a better fill. In fast moving markets, however, the market may move right past your price, resulting in your order not being executed. Here is an example of a limit order: "Buy one June T-bill at 92.05 or better." In

this case, since you have stated a price, your broker knows that this is a limit order.

(4) *Stop order*. A stop order to buy becomes a market order when the contract sells or is bid at or above the specified level; and if it is a sell order, it becomes a market order when the contract sells or is offered at or below the specified price. A buy stop must always be placed above the current trading level; and a sell stop, below it. Here is how it would work in our previous example on gold: "Buy one April gold at $400. Place an open protective sell stop at $380."

There are other types of fancy orders as well as numerous ways to combine them. A good reference book to have is *Commodity Futures Trading Orders* by J. R. Maxwell, Sr., 234 Main St., Red Bluff, CA 96080.

How To Get Started

A commonly asked question is: "How much money does it take to get started in the futures market?" The answer is that it depends on the brokerage firm with whom you are transacting business. Some brokerage firms will only ask for an initial deposit of $5,000; others may require $25,000 or more.

Once you open an account, a good rule of thumb is to have $4 in your account for every $1 that is margined. As an example, if the margin for copper is $1,200, you should have $4,800 in your account for each contract that you wish to trade. This is a conservative approach to futures trading. It is easy to get carried away and "overtrade" which can often be ruinous. The margin requirements change as the value of the contract increases or decreases in accordance with price or as the volatility of the contract changes.

Commissions

As in the stock market, commissions vary with the services of a brokerage firm. Full service brokerage firms have market research departments and offer fundamental and technical trading advice to their customers. Discount firms generally don't offer such services to their customers and, as a result, are able to reduce their commission rates. A single "round-turn" commission is charged to cover the trades you make to get in and out of each futures position. Unlike the stock market—where commission rates refer to either a buy or sell stock transaction—in the futures market, commissions are quoted on a "round-trip" basis—including both the purchase and sale. To receive a list of major brokerage firms dealing in the futures market, write to The Chicago Board of Trade, Marketing Department, LaSalle at Jackson, Chicago, IL 60604.

27

OPEN INTEREST

In the last chapter, we stated that investors and speculators in the futures market do not buy and sell actual goods or securities. Rather, they deal in *contracts*—an agreement which specifies that the seller will deliver to the buyer a quantity of a commodity or a financial instrument at a specific price on a specific date. *The number of contracts that are in existence at any given time is referred to as the "open interest."*

As a simple illustration, let's say you and I decide to start our own futures market to trade apples; and let's say we set as our standard that 100 bushels will equal one contract.

On the first day of trading, I agree that on December 20, I will deliver to you 500 bushels. You agree that you will buy from me those 500 bushels; and we each put down a small percentage of the total value as a guarantee.

In the parlance of the commodity markets, I have sold short 5 contracts of apples; while you have bought 5 contracts. What is the open interest so far? Very simple: 5 contracts.

Now let's move one step further. On the second day of trading, you get word from your friends in upstate New York that the apple crop is going to be huge this year, depressing the price. So you decide you want to sell out. But I don't know or don't care about that news and want to hold on to my 5 short positions. So, you sell out to a third party who assumes your contracts without affecting my position. The open interest is still five contracts.

However, on the third day of trading, several new buyers and new sellers enter the market, establishing 50 new short positions and 50 new long positions. Open interest increases to a total of 55.

What concerns us here, however, is not so much the absolute level of open interest but the patterns of change. For that purpose, we must define the four types of participants in the markets:

(1) *Old bulls* who have already bought and now hold long positions;

(2) *Old bears* who have already sold, and are now holding short positions;

(3) *New bulls* who are seeking to buy or are in the process of buying now; and

(4) *New bears* who are seeking to sell short or are in the process of selling short.

Try to visualize the market as an arena. Some investors are in the arena and have already made their commitments; while others are on the sidelines seeking to get in. But, remember, in every case, there is invariably one long position for every short position.

Why is it important that we watch open interest? Because by watching the change in open interest, we can often see if the market is strengthening or weakening.

IN A BULL MARKET, when an increase in open interest is accompanied by higher prices, it means that new buyers are continuing to enter the market. They are still willing to keep paying higher prices and, hence, continued strength can be expected.

When prices are still advancing but the open interest begins to go down, it means that new buying has stopped and that the buying being done is primarily by old bears who are exiting the market by covering their short positions. Meanwhile, the old bulls who held long positions are liquidating and taking profits. Therefore, *prices advancing but open interest declining is a signal that the price trend may be getting ready to reverse.*

After an uptrend has been under way for some time, open interest must be viewed in a different light. If the absolute level of open interest is extremely high, it indicates that there has been large public participation and that the market could be vulnerable. There probably are few buyers left on the sidelines who have not already bought and, thus, there is little chance open interest will continue to increase. Prices could fall rapidly should adverse news enter the market.

IN A BEAR MARKET, if prices are declining and open interest is increasing, it means that new bears are entering the market to sell short and, therefore, should continue to push prices lower.

But when open interest ceases to increase or begins to decline, it is a sign that the new bears are no longer willing to sell short at these lower prices. The selling that is taking place is primarily old bulls who are liquidating their long positions—an indication that the downward price movement may be coming to an end.

Some of the best work on open interest in commodities has been done by Jim Sibbet who publishes *Let's Talk Silver & Gold,* a market newsletter. Figure 27-1 shows Sibbet's "Eight Rules for Open Interest" which summarizes the effects of changing open interest on market conditions. Though these rules are widely accepted, my own research takes some exception to rules 3 and 4. Rather than neutral, when prices are moving sideways and open interest is rising we interpret this situation as bearish. When prices are moving sideways and open interest is falling our interpretation is bullish.

We would like to add the following considerations:

1. It is best not to try to interpret changes in open interest on a day-to-day basis. It is much more meaningful to watch for changes lasting from several days to a few weeks.

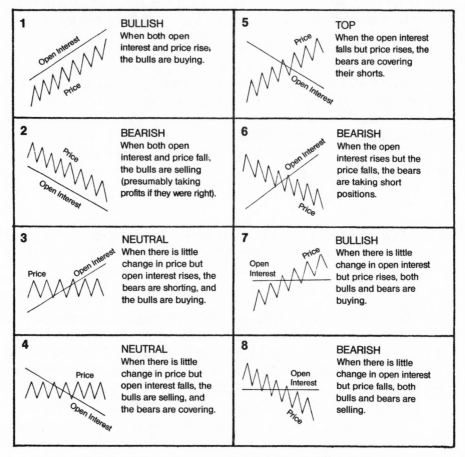

Reprinted from "Contrary Opinion," by R. Earl Hadady

Table 27-1

2. The open interest in many commodities tends to increase and decrease in a more or less fixed seasonal pattern. Therefore, any observed changes in open interest must be compared with the expected seasonal change.

The Commodity Research Bureau (CRB) publishes weekly graphs which display both the average open interest over the past few years and the current open interest, allowing you to detect the seasonal pattern.

Open interest should be compared to price activity on a daily or weekly basis:

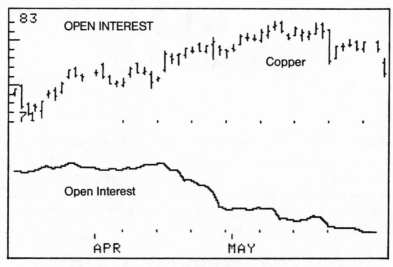

Figure 27-1

28

CONTRARY OPINION

The futures market is a "zero-sum game" in the sense that, for each contract outstanding, there is one long position and one short position and, therefore, there is invariably one losing contract for every winning contract. Due to this mandatory balance between buying and selling, contrary opinion plays an even greater role in future price direction than in the stock market.

Let's say we do a survey of market participants and find that 80% are bullish. How can 80% be bullish when each contract has a winner and a loser? Very simple! In this case, there are many bulls each holding — on the average—a relatively small number of contracts, whereas there are very few bears who must be holding a relatively large number.

The minority in the market, the 20% who are bearish in this instance, will most likely be well financed because they hold a large number of contracts. On the other hand, their opposition is probably lightly financed. Thus, the short positions are said to be in "strong hands" while the longs are in "weak hands" whose decisions are much more influenced by day-to-day price changes. A few adverse days will force them to liquidate their positions and retreat to the sidelines.

Continuing with our example, if 80% of the market participants are bulls, then the average trader who is long (a bull) holds only one-fourth as many contracts as the trader who is short (a bear). If only 10% are bulls, each bear holds on average 9 contracts for every one contract held by a bull.

How is the Bullish Consensus determined? It has been found that the overwhelming majority of commodity speculators follow the advice of various professionals who write market letters for brokerage firms or independent advisory services. Therefore, the trading attitude of the advisors will give us a good estimate of the public's bullishness or bearishness. Results have shown in most cases that if 90 percent of the professional advisors are bullish, then an overwhelming majority of the trading public will, likewise, be bullish.

HADADY PUBLICATIONS, (Imperial Savings Building, Suite 309, 61 South Lake Avenue, Pasadena, CA 91101) conducts a weekly survey of more than 100 of the leading brokerage firms and advisors. Earl Hadady is considered the Grand Master of Contrary Opinion in the commodity markets and has conducted extensive research in the field. You can obtain several years' history of Bullish Consensus readings from him, build a file, and run your own tests on the data (see figure 28-1). Another less ambitious alternative would be to subscribe to his chart service which graphs the Bullish Consensus for each commodity at the bottom of the chart.

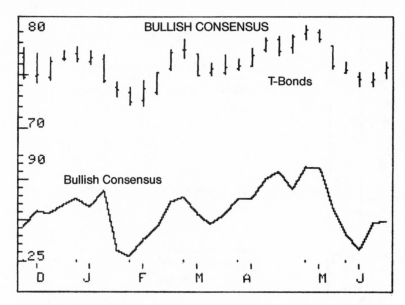

Figure 28-1

To rate the significance of a Bullish Consensus reading, refer to Hadady's Bullish Consensus Meter   (Figure 28-2).

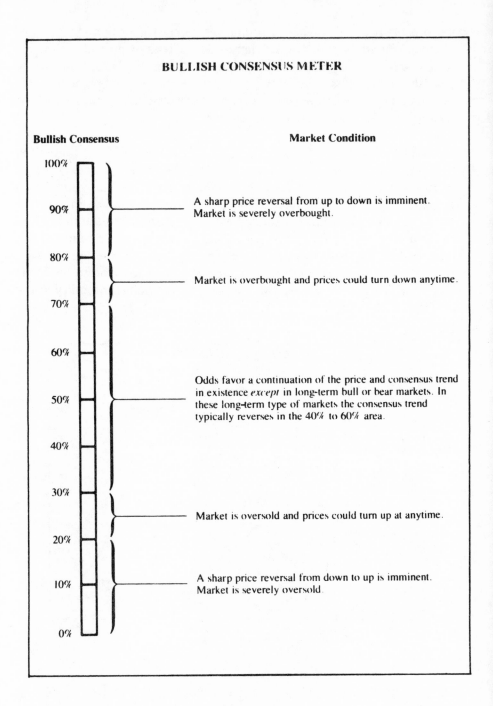

BULLISH CONSENSUS METER

Bullish Consensus

Market Condition

100%

90% — A sharp price reversal from up to down is imminent. Market is severely overbought.

80%

70% — Market is overbought and prices could turn down anytime.

60%

50% — Odds favor a continuation of the price and consensus trend in existence *except* in long-term bull or bear markets. In these long-term type of markets the consensus trend typically reverses in the 40% to 60% area.

40%

30% — Market is oversold and prices could turn up at anytime.

20%

10% — A sharp price reversal from down to up is imminent. Market is severely oversold.

0%

Figure 28-2

An "overbought" condition begins to occur when the Bullish Consensus exceeds 80%; an "oversold" condition when the consensus is less than 30%. A contrarian position should be considered any time the Bullish Consensus is above 80% or below 30%. The probability for a successful contrarian trade increases as the Bullish Consensus approaches the extremes, i.e. 100% and 0%. When the Bullish Consensus percentages are in the ranges of 80 - 90% or 20 - 30%, it is advisable to wait until the trend of the Bullish Consensus reverses direction before entering a position. For a more in-depth study of contrary opinion, we recommend Earl Hadady's *Contrary Opinion,* Hadady Publications, Pasadena, CA 91101.

29

SHORT-TERM TECHNICAL INDICATORS

Because of greater volatility and higher leverage, the futures markets generally require more precise timing of trades than is necessary in the stock market. In the stock market, several days of adverse action can easily be tolerated and may not affect a long-term trade. This, of course, is not the case in the futures markets, where a few days could easily produce a margin call and do catastrophic damage to an account. A good knowledge of Part II will provide the necessary tools to allow you to master short-term timing techniques. The following two short-term indicators are among my favorites. Used properly, they can often identify market tops and bottoms to a day, thus allowing you to enter trades with a limited risk.

Demand Index

THE DEMAND INDEX, developed by Jim Sibbet, (Sibbet Publications, 61 S. Lake Ave., Pasadena, CA 91101), uses a copyrighted formula and, therefore, cannot be reproduced in this book. However, Computrac (with Mr. Sibbet's permission) does offer the indicator as part of their package. The index combines volume and price data in such a way as to become a leading indicator of a price trend change. It is designed so that at the very least it is a coincidental indicator, not a lagging one. This is based on the general observation that volume tends to peak before prices, both in the commodity and stock markets.

The best way to use it is to look for a divergence between the index and prices.

If prices are moving lower or have made a lower bottom while the Demand Index is moving higher or has made a higher bottom, this is called bullish divergence and prices should move higher:

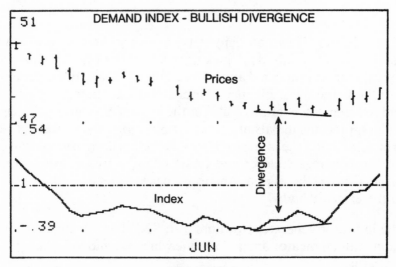

Figure 29-1

If prices are moving higher or have made a higher top while the Demand Index is moving lower or has made a lower top, this is called bearish divergence and signifies that prices should move lower:

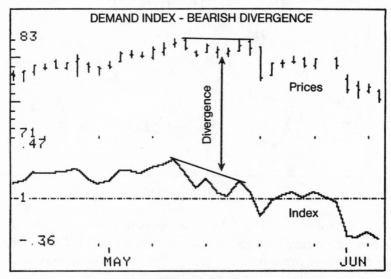

Figure 29-2

Thus, the Demand Index can be used to identify both market tops and market bottoms.

Stochastic Process

This indicator, if run on daily data, is a very short-term oriented but highly accurate method for picking tops and bottoms. We find it can be a great market timing aid and often employ it when making recommendations on the Weiss Financial Futures Hotline which gives specific buy and sell recommendations daily for the interest rate futures, foreign currencies, precious metals markets and other futures markets. The basic principle behind the indicator is this: As prices decrease, the daily closes tend to congregate closer and closer to the extreme lows of the daily range. Conversely, as prices increase, the closes tend to congregate closer to the extreme *highs*.

The indicator generates two lines—an "X" line which is a short-term momentum indicator and a "Y" line which is a moving average of that indicator:

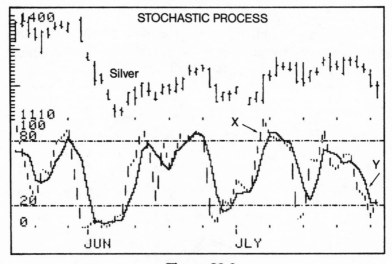

Figure 29-3

The indicator is used much like the Demand Index. The major formation to be looking for is *a divergence between the Y line on the model and the actual price on your chart*. This divergence may take one of two forms: bullish divergence or bearish divergence.

1. *Bullish divergence* occurs when the actual price makes a lower low but the Y line fails to break to new low ground. Your confirmation and signal to buy—immediately—is given on the day that the X line crosses up through the Y line (Figure 29-4).

2. Referring to figure 29-5, a *bearish divergence* occurs when the actual price makes a higher top yet the Y line has correspondingly failed to do so. Your confirmation and signal to *sell*—immediately—is given on the day that the X line crosses *down* through the Y line.

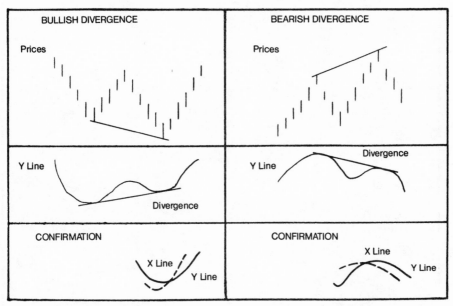

Figure 29-4   **Figure 29-5**

How accurate is the indicator in picking tops and bottoms? In order to judge its ability for yourself, review the Daily Chart on the T-bills extending from October 1981 through June 1982 (figure 29-6). Here are the signals it gave:

(1) The first sell signal was generated on November 30, 1981. Notice that the Y line peaked on November 12 and continued to move lower, while prices moved higher over the next two weeks, setting up our basic divergence. On November 30, the X line crashed down through the lower

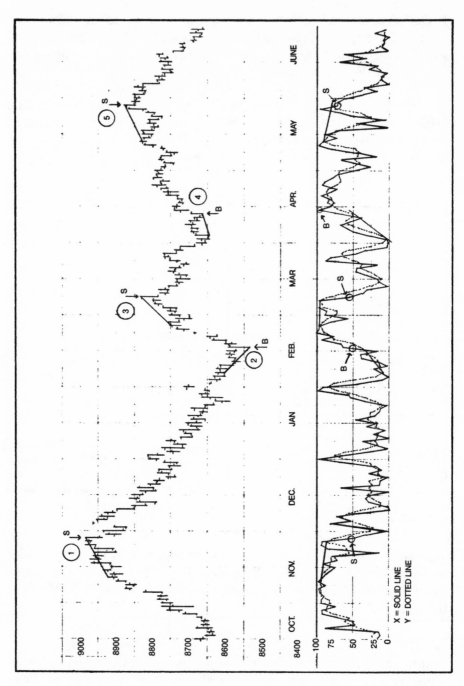

Figure 29-6

top made by the Y line and gave us our signal to sell. Prices fell sharply from that point.

(2) Our first buy signal was generated February 16, 1982—the exact day of the bottom. Notice how the Y line had been rising from February 4, while prices continued to decline, setting up our divergence. On February 16, the X line crossed through the Y line, giving us our buy signal.

(3) The next sell signal was given at the peak of the intermediate top made on March 8, 1982. Prices were moving higher from February 24 to March 8, while the Y line made a slightly lower top on March 5. On March 8, the X line crossed down through the Y line, generating the sell signal.

(4) A good buy signal was again flashed on April 8, 1982. Note that although both prices and the Y line were moving up, the Y line moved much more rapidly, still setting up a divergence.

(5) Another perfect sell signal was given *at the exact top* made on May 21, 1982. Divergence had been set up from higher peaks made in prices on May 21 over May 7, while correspondingly lower peaks were made on the Y line.

Again, remember to never rely on one indicator alone and to always use stops. When using this indicator to buy, place a stop just below the most recent low. When using the indicator to sell short, place a stop just above the most recent high.

30

MONEY MANAGEMENT

It is only natural when we make an investment or trade that we tend to focus on potential profits rather than dwell on possible losses. We are often so convinced that a particular trade will be profitable that we tend to push to the back of our minds thoughts that something could go awry. But in order to be successful traders, we must face these thoughts head-on. Losing trades are inevitable. It is how we manage and control those losses that eventually determines our success in the markets.

Money management is simply an assortment of techniques that help a trader minimize the risk of loss while still enabling him to participate in major market gains. Ironically, it is very possibly the most critical aspect of futures trading *and* the most overlooked. Whereas stock market investors can sometimes get by without it, in futures markets because of the high leverage available, it is an absolute must! Without the implementation of strict loss-control techniques, sudden catastrophic losses can quickly shrink an account to such an extreme that the possibility of ever attaining profitability becomes remote.

Once a trader fully understands this concept, he has probably learned the most important lesson in trading. Specifically: *The percent gain needed to recover a loss increases geometrically with the loss*. For example, if you lose 15% of your capital, you have to make a 17.6% gain on the balance you have left to get even. If you lose 30% of your capital, it will take a 42.9% gain; and if you lose 50% of your capital, it will take 100%. The following table illustrates this point.

TABLE 30-1. RECOVERY TABLE

% Loss Of Initial Capital	% Gain On Balance Required To Recover loss
5	5.3
10	11.1
15	17.6
20	25.0
25	33.3
30	42.9
35	53.8
40	66.7
45	81.8
50	100.0
55	122.0
60	150.0
65	186.0
70	233.0
75	300.0
80	400.0
85	567.0
90	900.0

Hopefully, the table has impressed upon you the fact that preservation of capital is of utmost importance. But exactly how do we go about doing that? A good place to start is to always predetermine an exit point (a stop) *before* you enter a trade.

The stop should meet two requirements. First, it should be "logical" from a technical standpoint. For example, if you are "long," a stop under a previous support area would be logical. Second, and even more important, the stop should be a function of money management—that is, how much you can afford to risk on a particular trade. Certain rules of thumb exist such as limiting your risk to 10% of total capital on any one trade. But such rules are often too general to be of much use. If you employ a trading system, your losses will automatically be limited as a function of the system. Thus, you will not have to define a stop for each trade; the system does it for you. For example, a moving average crossover system will automatically prevent catastrophic losses. Of course, a series of smaller losses could still wipe out your account, but at least you are giving the law of averages an opportunity to work for you.

I. Lee Finberg, a specialist in managed accounts for Prudential-Bache and a frequent public speaker on money management principles, writing in *Money Maker* magazine (December/January 1983) adds the following warning: "Don't stay with unprofitable positions. In futures markets, exiting from unprofitable positions while the loss is relatively small is a must because of the effects of leverage when your position or timing proves wrong."

The proprietary Delta Strategy we've designed for our clients at Weiss Money Management—in conjunction with our weekly econometric model—also pays credence to the old adage: "Cut your losses and let profits run"; and, in practice, it has worked to our advantage. Whenever the market begins moving adversely to the position, the position is automatically exited.

This is the way most trend-following systems work. By testing the system on several years of past data on each of the markets you intend to trade, you can determine how much back-up money you will need for each contract traded by calculating the "drawdown." This refers to the maximum dollar loss suffered during the test period. Here is a simple example:

TABLE 30-2. DRAWDOWNS

Beginning Balance		$10,000
Trade #1	+$2,000	$12,000
Trade #2	+$1,000	$13,000
Trade #3	+$4,000	$17,000
Trade #4	-$6,000	$11,000
Trade #5	+$3,000	$14,000
Trade #6	-$8,000	$ 6,000
Trade #7	+$2,000	$ 8,000
Trade #8	+$5,000	$13,000
Trade #9	+$2,000	$15,000
Trade #10	+$5,000	$20,000

At first glance, this example appears to show a profitable track record. The account went from $10,000 to $20,000 after 10 trades. But what would have occurred if your beginning trade was Trade #4?

TABLE 30-3. DRAWDOWNS

Beginning Balance		$10,000
Trade #4	-$6,000	$ 4,000
Trade #5	+$3,000	$ 7,000
Trade #6	-$8,000	WIPED OUT!

You would never have reached the profit zone—let alone the $20,000 -- because the "drawdown" was too great. Thus, this system is either unworkable or must be capitalized to a greater degree. For instance, had you begun your account with $20,000 rather than $10,000, you would have ended up with a $10,000 or 50% profit and a workable system.

When testing our system one market at a time, we've found approximately four dollars was required for each one dollar margined to assure that the account would not be decimated by drawdowns. For example, a market requiring a $2,000 margin would require an $8,000 beginning account.

However, when we assumed that all nine markets were being traded simultaneously we found that the maximum drawdown was greatly reduced. The reason is simple: While some markets are losing money, others are profiting, thereby smoothing out the overall performance. In our case, we found that when the Weiss Money Management portfolio was completely diversified, the back-up margin required was reduced from $1 to a ratio of $1.20 to $1. Since far less initial capital was needed, our potential – and actual—yield was greatly multiplied. Needless to say, therefore, *portfolio diversification*, if possible, is highly desirable. It has been proven mathematically and is worth remembering.

The following is a summary of the important points you should keep in mind regarding money management:

1. Avoid large capital losses.

2. Use stops that are "logical" and also a function of money management.

3. Use a trading system if possible.

4. Be adequately capitalized.

5. Be aware of the extent of potential drawdowns.

6. Diversify your portfolio.

Conclusion

Interviews with successful self-made men and women reveal a common theme—a willingness to work hard, and a willingness to take risks. Though these two qualities cannot guarantee success, the lack of either one will more than likely preclude it.

True success stories in the stock and commodity markets, while not unheard of, are at least a rarity. This unfortunate circumstance can be quite easily explained. The vast majority of the investing public, lacking the time and expertise to analyze markets on their own, instead tend to follow what others are doing—the "herd instinct." This usually results in "lemmings into the sea."

Two Wall Street truisms are apropos: "The majority is always wrong" and "If it is obvious, it is obviously wrong."

It is a frustrating fact that a simple survey of price changes in stocks, options and especially the highly leveraged "futures" markets over a period of time reveals to even the casual observer that fortunes could be made if one could make market decisions that were just slightly more right than wrong. Yet the majority of the investing public continues to lose money in the stock and commodity markets.

This occurs because: (1) most investors do not take the time to learn how to analyze markets on their own and thus are forced to rely on others' opinions—tips and rumors, and (2) they allow their emotions to play too much of a role in their decision making. This book will, hopefully, allow you to overcome these problems and make you successful in the stock and commodity markets.

You are now taking control and have taken the first step toward breaking away from the crowd.

EPILOGUE

EPILOGUE

TOMORROW'S VISTAS

In the beginning of this book, we visited the past. Now as we come to the end, let us project ourselves into the twenty-first century. Based on our experiences of the 1980s, some might expect to see either a great collapse or tremendous growth, either a kind of "dark ages," or a supersociety of supercasinos in every financial marketplace. Instead, we are shocked to discover that it is *entirely different from anything we had ever imagined.* We walk into the nearest brokerage/banking building and resolve to find out what we can.

Our first discovery is that the twentieth-century trend towards specialization of professions has been reversed; when we ask to see a technical analyst we are introduced to an individual who is also a social scientist and historian.

"Uhm, we've been kind of 'out of it' for the past thirty years. Could you please fill us in on what's happened?"

Slowly but surely, the answers begin to pour forth: "The last two decades of the twentieth century," he tells us "brought first boom and then bust throughout the four corners of the globe. But that was merely part and parcel of what we call *'the great transformation.'* The 1980s, in particular, were among the strangest and most turbulent times in recent memory, times when nothing was sacred; 'normal' had no apparent meaning; everything was in a state of flux."

"You're not telling me anything new."

"No. But what most market analysts of those days didn't realize is that, in the long-term perspective of history, the .OP chaos was merely a temporary phenomenon—symptoms of a quantum leap in social and economic evolution. Meanwhile, what escaped the attention of most historians and social scientists of the day was the fact that the epicenter of *this evolutionary process was none other than the financial markets.*"

"Please be more specific."

"OK. Let me put it this way: The great transformation has brought three major changes.

"First, we no longer have a distinct dichotomy between investors and noninvestors, speculators vs. commercials, or winners vs. losers. We are beyond the era when markets were largely a zero-sum game, where one person's bonanza was another person's disaster. Personal computers, then home computers, and finally pocket or wrist computers have been great equalizers, giving virtually everyone the data they need to make rational decisions. The more information, the fewer the surprises, and the smaller the resulting market gyrations."

"So anyone who didn't know computers got left behind, eh?"

"Actually, it often turned out the other way around. It was those who got bogged down in the intricacies of computer technology and programming languages that sometimes missed the boat. The swifter road to success was to learn how to use a wide variety of 'user friendly' programs.

"The second major change has been the development of **artificial intelligence,** the ability of computers to learn and reprogram themselves in dynamic interaction with market events. In the 1980s, artificial intelligence was still in its infancy. Now, it is said to be in its 'childhood.' No matter how far it develops, however, I can assure you that human beings will remain firmly in control. The idea of computers taking over the world is, and always will be, science fiction simply because man 's intelligence is evolving so much faster."

"But what is the aim of artificial intelligence—to predict and control the future?"

"On a very low level, yes, sometimes. But when you gain control on one level, the critical social and economic events begin to occur on a higher level where you cannot exert control ... which leads me to the last and most important change: In the past it was believed that we had reached the point where we could control, by government mandate, the price of money, labor or goods.

"Now, after our second great depression as a world power, we are far more humble. We recognize the inevitability of cycles and long waves. So rather than trying to prevent their occurrence by sticking our fingers in the dike or by sweeping the dirt under the rug, we attempt to ride with them, and if we're especially ambitious, to somehow round off the valleys *as well as the peaks*.

"We've also recognized that these cycles and rhythms of nature are not merely external. As a species, all human beings do indeed march to the beat of the same drummer; are all part of, and responsive to, the same circadian universals."

"So?"

"We have learned to monitor and to measure these internal human rhythms ... especially as they relate to markets, and to *profits,*" he concluded with a half smile. But sensing we didn't quite understand, he continued: "In other words, we have been able to overcome much of the fear, the unfounded hopes, the unbridled greed that plagued investors of the past ... to focus on the results of our technical analysis with objectivity ... and exercise a great deal more personal discipline.

"It has been the combination of these three changes—a more harmonious coexistence with the natural waves and cycles, a broader participation by the average man in the information networks, and the development of artificial intelligence—which has brought us the one thing we cherish the most: price stability."

"Sounds too good to be true."

"Granted, now the volatility and uncertainty is in areas that didn't even exist in the last century, but ... that would take months to explain."

"I see. So to be a speculator must be tough these days."

"Yes. I guess you could say that. In order to generate substantial profits out of the relatively narrower price fluctuations, you would need much more leverage than in the old days; and, at the same time, credit is not quite as abundant. Back in those days, as uncertainty mounted, the time perspective of most investors shortened—from years to months, to days and sometimes just minutes. Today, the opposite has occurred.

"Some things, however, never change. Great discoveries are eternal ... no one has ever really written a better geometry than Euclid for example. Likewise, many of the principles discovered and developed by the great technical analysts of the twentieth century have stood the test of time."

"Such as?"

"Moving averages, retracement theory, support and resistance, and the significance of accumulation and distribution, to name but a few, are equally as valuable today as before. All we've done, essentially, is to combine them into integrated computer models which simultaneously resolve thousands of interrelated equations."

"Yes, but what I want to know is who are the winners and who are the losers?"

"The problem today is as it was then; if you have two men and one of them has a gun, the man with the gun has the advantage ... until the other guy goes out and gets a gun of his own to even things up. With technical analysis, when everyone has the same tools, the final differential, the ultimate arbitrator of success, becomes the skills of the individual technician."

INDEX

READER SERVICES: THREE GRATIS REPORTS
PREPARED ESPECIALLY FOR THE READERS OF THIS BOOK

The boundaries of technical analysis continue to press forward. This is because the field of technical analysis is heavily populated with innovative "technical tinkerers," and other creative individuals that are constantly striving to improve the reliability -- hence the profitability -- of the various indicators and techniques that you have learned about in this book. As a gratis service to our readers, and as a valuable part of your continuing education, Weiss Research publishes:

(1) **Timing The Market Updates.** These are periodic updates that will help you "keep your finger on the pulse" of: * new developments * new technical analysis techniques * new indicators and trading systems that have recently burst onto the scene.

(2) **The Delta Strategy (36-page booklet).** We also anticipate that many of you might wonder exactly how a systematic program of investing via technical analysis might be constructed. Weiss Research has just completed work on such a project, which we call the *Delta Strategy.* You may find it interesting to see how we have integrated the principles and techniques in this book into the architecture of a trading system that is currently being successfully utilized in the markets. An actual copy of *The Delta Strategy* is available to you. We give you complete permission to use any of the information, techniques, formulas, and theories contained in the *Delta Strategy* as you see fit.

(3) **Computerizing Your Technical Analysis (25-page booklet).** Last but not least, since the scope of this book didn't allow for a more complete discussion on the use, impact, and selection of computers and computer programs for technical analysis, we have prepared a special report on computerized investing that will help you to enter this critical arena with confidence. This factual report covers (among other things): Selecting software; selecting hardware; and how to build a stock and commodity database. It also includes a list of vendors for some difficult-to-locate services and products.

All of these reports are gratis to readers of this book. Simply make your selection below, print your name and address and enclose $2.00 for each report you select to cover postage and handling.

Mail to: WEISS RESEARCH, INC.
        P.O. Box 2923
        West Palm Beach. FL   33402

Please send me the item(s) I have checked below. I am enclosing $2.00 each to cover postage and handling.

Name _____

Street _____

State _____ Zip _____

☐ 1. TIMING THE MARKET UPDATES

☐ 2. THE DELTA STRATEGY

☐ 3. COMPUTERIZING YOUR TECHNICAL ANALYSIS